A Companion to the Anglican Liturgy

This is the Feast

Words, music and resources for making Holy Week happen

Michael Forster and
Robert B. Kelly

Kevin Mayhew

First published in 1996 by
KEVIN MAYHEW LTD.
Rattlesden
Bury St Edmunds
Suffolk IP30 0SZ

0 1 2 3 4 5 6 7 8 9

ISBN 0 86209 918 8
Catalogue No 1500082

Front cover: *The Morning of the Resurrection* (oil on panel), by Sir Edward Burne-Jones (1838-1898).
Reproduced by courtesy of Christie's Images/Bridgeman Art library, London

Cover design by Graham Johnstone
Edited by Geoffrey Peachey
Typesetting by Louise Hill
Printed and bound in Great Britain

Contents

Introduction

The climax of the church's liturgical year, the feast around which all the other feasts are arranged, the heart and soul of all our sacramental celebrations: the Paschal Vigil.

As the central feast, when we celebrate the fullness of the Paschal Mystery of Christ's death, resurrection and glorification, it should be no surprise to find that throughout history this feast has been given special attention and reverence by the church.

For that reason, much of the material – and many of the references – included in this book reflect how the liturgical practices familiar to present-day congregations actually spring from very ancient practices in which all Christian denominations are rooted, but which have since become associated with particular traditions. Rather than being an obstacle, we hope this may enable and encourage a re-evaluation of symbols and rites, both those already familiar and those that may have become unfamiliar.

It is not the purpose of this book to impose ideas, but to offer resources which, in turn, do not demand to be accepted *en bloc* but may be used selectively to enhance and enrich, rather than to supersede the familiar patterns in individual parishes.

Historically, the church's respect for the Paschal Vigil has been shown by two, seemingly paradoxical tendencies:

- wanting to respect the most ancient traditions
- yet always seeking out new ways in which to express better what is being celebrated.

That is why the church has *always* celebrated the Paschal Vigil – what Augustine called 'the mother of all vigils'.

So it is that, to allow time to meditate on and to appreciate the different aspects of this Paschal Mystery, the Vigil grew into what we now call the 'Paschal Triduum', that is, the three-day celebration, Thursday-Friday-Saturday.

This Triduum is constituted in part by what used to belong to the one celebration at the Vigil: elements which had served as the Liturgy of the Word for the all-night Vigil were shared out across the other days. In particular, what used to be the Gospel of the Vigil, the proclamation of Christ's passion and resurrection according to John, has been moved to Good Friday (and shortened, because originally on the Saturday it was read as far as John 20:17, alluding to the ascension). So too, the Exodus reading now used at the Maundy Thursday eucharist was once part of the Saturday Vigil of readings.

At the climax of the Vigil, in the early church as today, came the celebration of the sacraments of initiation: baptism-confirmation-eucharist, by which each Christian shares sacramentally in the Paschal Mystery of Christ and its redemptive power, here and now; which is why the liturgy constantly uses the present tense: 'This is the feast . . .', 'This is the night . . .'.

The elements that have been added to Holy Week came principally from Jerusalem, where the presence of so many actual sites of the historic events of these last days of Christ's life gave a particular shape and colour to their ceremonies. From Jerusalem we inherit the procession of palms on Palm Sunday; the evening celebration of the eucharist on the Thursday; Good Friday's commemoration of Christ's passion, with the great solemn prayers of intercession and the proclamation of the cross.

Pilgrims to Jerusalem were so impressed by these processions and ceremonies that when they got back home they introduced them into their own liturgy, thus creating what we now call Holy Week.

But as well as these Jerusalem influences, elements have been borrowed from Greek traditions, and indeed from the Celtic tradition. Anyone who has read the lives of Saint Patrick or Saint Columba will have no trouble in recognising the sacred bonfire which now opens the Saturday celebration.

Christians throughout history did not think they were doing anything shocking in such reworking, borrowing and innovating. They simply dared to take Easter seriously and constantly sought better ways to express its significance in readings, songs, gestures and rites: to try and make it in *reality* as well as in *principle*, their greatest feast.

This book sees itself in the same bold but unpretentious tradition. Our starting point is always the Paschal Mystery whose celebration lies at the heart of Holy Week. Thereafter, it asks simply, how can this or that part of these liturgies be celebrated, taking account of the concrete reality of the average parish, with its limited resources, its busy people, in today's world. For we authors, both are important: *what* is to be celebrated, and *who* is going to do the celebrating.

We both have pastoral experience of magnificent Holy Week celebrations; but experience also tells us that such grandiose events are often inappropriate to the local setting and the resources available. Even when this is not the case, such necessarily specialised music is often at the unacceptable cost of excluding the people from taking their full and active part. During Holy Week, the people should be participants, not mere spectators, which means the music needs, for the most part, to be known, accessible and able to be sung well without rehearsal.

Hence this book, whose roots are twofold:

- the tradition of the church and the magnificent collection of texts, gestures and rites which can create the appropriate atmosphere for meditation on and celebration of the Paschal Mystery
- the awareness of the ordinary parish's sincere will and instinct to celebrate well, yet at the same time with perhaps only limited resources for celebration.

Respecting these two considerations has been achieved by studying and reworking the rich heritage the tradition of the church offers, so that the key moments of this week's liturgy can be celebrated in song to tunes already known to the people. The tunes have been chosen according to a double principle:

- their appropriateness to the message of the text and the mood of the liturgical moment (a stirring tune for the Canticle of Moses, Exodus 15; the classic Bach *Passion Chorale* for the song for the procession to the altar of repose, *Finlandia* for the Reproaches, etc.)
- that they are already well-known tunes, so that everyone in the congregation is able to reclaim the liturgical texts which are rightfully theirs and can proclaim them in song with ease.

This is a practice with a very long history in the liturgy. We know, for example, that Ambrose, as well as composing, wrote new words to existing tunes for his congregations, but carefully explains why some kinds of tune (for example because of their pagan overtones) were unsuitable.

Perhaps he saw nothing shocking in the idea because he was so familiar with the psalms. A good example of this is Psalm 22 (the psalm for Good Friday). If we look it up in a reliable translation, we find that before the verses proper begin there is a direction such as 'according to the Doe of Dawn'. In other words, the psalm was written to be sung to a pre-existing, familiar song which had that title. Other examples are both Psalms 45 and 69 to the tune 'Lilies'; Psalms 57-9 to the tune 'Do not destroy'.

Hereafter, we explain, first in general terms and then for each individual day, how what we offer might be used. In every case our aim is to make a particular liturgical moment come alive, to be a space for prayer, to allow an opportunity for deeper understanding or appreciation of the Paschal Mystery.

The test will be if our assemblies come away feeling, 'Yes, indeed, this really is *the* feast . . .'.

MICHAEL FORSTER AND ROBERT KELLY

General Principles

How to Use this Book

1. Use this book as much as you need to, but **only** *as much as you need to.*

This book is designed to facilitate the creative celebration of Holy Week: to help, rather than dispense with preparation. We cannot imagine that any parish will want slavishly to implement all that this book offers.

This first principle may seem a little strange, given the time and energy we have devoted to putting the resources together. However, it is quite simply the natural corollary of what prompted us to do so. If we are offering a resource for parishes which are 'over-stretched', by the same token it would be deeply regrettable if parishes took the 'easy way out' and 'under-stretched' themselves.

A parish which invests effort and creativity in getting its Easter celebration right will reap rewards which stretch beyond Holy Week, giving added sense and dynamism to the whole liturgical year. Sadly, the opposite is also true. A parish which skimps in its efforts to make Easter special is betraying an incomplete if not inadequate appreciation of the Paschal Mystery, and whose year-round celebrations of the eucharist and the other sacraments will be the poorer.

However, we need to be realistic about what can be achieved.

A judicious use of this book will allow the choice of one or two, even several 'new' pieces of liturgical music, so that energy can be concentrated on using them to maximum effect.

Let us imagine you have found a motet – one of those by Vittoria for *Tenebrae*, for example – that would make a splendid meditation on Christ's passion for Good Friday: let the choir dedicate their time to mastering it, so that when they come to sing it not only are all the notes right but the music makes the words come alive for the people. Meantime, you can dedicate that time to it because you know that other, equally important moments will be served by the texts offered here, sung to appropriate tunes that the congregation already know. Again, the music – albeit familiar – will be the servant of the text, and the opportunity for the assembly to 'chew over' and assimilate the word.

Or again, you may have one or more gifted soloists whose God-given talent will enrich your celebrations, for example in psalms that suit the style and range of their voices, so that the sung proclamation of the psalms, the word of God, moves the people to respond better to the readings they have heard.

2. *Celebrate the Paschal Mystery*

No matter what day of Holy Week, no matter what moment of that day, the underlying point is always to celebrate, and thereby render effective here and now, Christ's saving Paschal Mystery.

Consequently, there is an essential unity to the whole of Holy Week. As we said in the introduction, in the early church there was nothing but the Easter Vigil, as the unified, complete celebration of Christ's passion, death, resurrection and glorification. The fact that we now have it spread across several days is not to celebrate different bits of it at different times, but simply to give us more time to appreciate this overall mystery, by regarding it from different facets.

The people will appreciate this fundamental unity instinctively if those responsible for the organisation of the week's liturgies consciously seek to express it through the various complementarities and the symmetries that exist between the different days.

An example of this can be found in a tradition which, although unfamiliar in many parishes, may perhaps be worthy of consideration. At least three of the days might involve some or all of the congregation in special processions:

- with palms on the Sunday;
- to venerate the cross on the Friday;
- following the Paschal candle at the Vigil.

It is well worth trying to shape the processions so that they follow (at least partly) the same physical route, helping the people appreciate that each time they are being invited to process as a public and active profession of their faith in one and the same Paschal Mystery:

- on Sunday as an expression of their belief in Christ as Messiah;
- on Friday to proclaim the triumph of the cross;
- at the Vigil, to acclaim the risen Lord and express their willingness to be guided by him.

The words we offer for the processional songs were designed with this in mind.

This is why the *Agnus Dei* this book offers has the same tune, and some common verses, for Palm Sunday, Maundy Thursday and Good Friday – while at the same time allowing a specific meditation on how each of those days clarifies in its own way that very mysterious title which John the Baptist gave Jesus, 'the Lamb of God'.

Whatever we do on each of the days of Holy Week needs to be built on the foundation of the fundamental unity of the Paschal Mystery. We people of western culture are not helped in this regard by having a very 'chronological' vision of things, which can work against a healthy appreciation of sacramental mysteries (for example, how many people get distracted by a pointless question such as 'at what point does the bread become Christ's body?').

There is a danger that we compartmentalise the Paschal Mystery in terms of historic moments, and think that on Good Friday we celebrate Christ's death and at Easter his resurrection. The church has never celebrated anything but the Paschal Mystery, whole and entire: the mystery of his passing through death and resurrection to glorification, and into which same saving mystery he invites all humankind. Thereafter, to help our appreciation of this single but complex mystery, we commemorate different features of it at different moments. Thus, while Good Friday celebrates the triumph of the cross, it commemorates the cost of that triumph: Christ's passion and death.

But this does not mean our Good Friday liturgy has to pretend we do not know that Christ is risen! All our Christian tradition, including scripture itself and all the sacraments, are post-paschal. It is inescapably as Easter people that we gaze upon the cross and try to fathom its mystery. Our Easter faith presses back into our understanding of Good Friday, to enlarge and transform it. But equally, our experience of the cross – yes, we are meant to *experience* it – informs and shapes our Easter faith.

The chronological disposition of the feasts of Holy Week is secondary; what is important is that the liturgy plunges us with Christ into his death so that with him we may rise again. This is why the sacraments of initiation have their truest place at the Easter Vigil. We ought to be rejoicing in our God-given post-resurrection faith, which should enable us to face the reality of the cross from 'this' side of Easter at least as faithfully as Jesus faced it from the 'wrong' side of Easter!

It is from this perspective of the risen Paschal Christ that the evangelist John opens the passion, as far back as John chapter 13 (especially in verses 31-32). For Paul, 'the Lord' is always the risen Christ. However, to combat the all too superficial enthusiasm of his converts who were so full of the resurrection that they forgot the cross, Paul utters a whole series of reminders – even to the extent of inventing words which did not exist in Greek to express this: we are 'co-crucified'. Even so, for Paul, the essence of the cross is its role in the Paschal Mystery (into which our 'co-crucifixion' thrusts us), which is why he calls on us 'to *glory* in the cross of Christ' (Galatians 6:14).

If Good Friday is not and never has been the celebration of *only* Christ's death, neither was the Vigil ever the celebration of *only* his resurrection. Originally the passion according to John was the Gospel for this liturgy. With typical precision, the Preface from the Vigil summarises succinctly what we celebrate: '. . . this night when *Christ became our paschal sacrifice*'.

We are called, then, to celebrate a passover, a paschal sacrifice, a process which transcends history, not a series of historical events. By all means let our commemoration of specific time-bound moments facilitate our celebration, but only so as better to celebrate, bring alive for us here and now, the unique, indivisible, even if complex, Paschal Mystery of our redemption.

3. Know each day, each moment, what it is you want to celebrate!

This third principle follows from the second: once the firm vision has been set of one single week-long celebration of the same Paschal Mystery, then the purpose of each day, and indeed of each of the liturgical moments of each day – because each day in itself is a complex web of references and allusions, words and gestures – can be defined.

In other words, clear planning is needed:

- how this day fits in with the rest of what is being done in Holy Week
- what facet of the Paschal Mystery this day is going to explore and lay before the people
- how the particular part of the liturgy for that day contributes to the meaning of the day, how it complements the other rites of that same day (and therefore how it relates to the other days).

If the ideas are clear enough, they should each be able to be expressed in a phrase.

It may be easier to understand in terms of an example – even if this does mean anticipating a little on what follows in the particular chapters.

Holy Saturday invites us to celebrate the *Passover* of Christ.

Thereafter, the celebration is divided into four main

parts, each of which offers a symbolic expression, in word, song and gesture, of that central theme of *Passover*:

- in the Liturgy of Light, we *pass* from darkness to light, we *pass* from outside the building to inside
- in the Liturgy of the Word we hear how the world *passes* from nothingness into being, how the Hebrew slaves *pass* through the sea to freedom, etc
- in the Liturgy of Baptism, by *passing* through water, we *pass* with Christ into the tomb of death so as to *pass over* and rise with him to new life
- in the Liturgy of the Eucharist, what is merely bread and wine *passes* into being Christ's body and blood; we who participate *pass* from being simply a collection of people into being the Body of Christ.

For confirmation of this, we need look no further than the Collect for Easter Eve:

> 'Grant, Lord,
> that we who are baptised into the death of your Son our Saviour Jesus Christ
> may continually put to death our evil desires and be buried with him;
> that through the grave and gate of death
> we may pass to our joyful resurrection;
> through his merits, who died and was buried and rose again for us,
> your Son Jesus Christ our Lord.'

As liturgy planners we now need to decide, how can what we do and sing express the *Passover* in each of these *passages*? How can what we sing help inspire the 'confidence' that the Vigil is designed to instil in us? How can what we sing help us to *pass* out of the church at the end of the celebration back into the world, renewed, changed, charged with the Spirit, motivated to work for the ultimate *Passover*, the coming of the Kingdom?

The authors of this book come from two different denominational traditions, from two different spiritual cultures, even. But none of the texts offered here was drafted until we had worked out a common vision of each liturgical moment. Sometimes it appeared deceptively easy – the purpose of the rite seemed self-evident – but our dialogue proved there is always more to discover, that rites always work on several levels. Other rites demanded deeper probing, as we each tried to view them from the other's perspective. Neither of us 'compromised', but from the strength of our respective traditions, we enriched one another's understanding of the purpose of each rite and its traditional text.

We believe that each parish has the same task, which should be easier to the extent that by definition the members of the congregation are more likely all to belong to the same denomination! But the underlying challenge remains the same: to know *what* is being celebrated, *what* the church wants to be celebrated, and the shaping of the *how* will become far more self-evident.

4. Whatever resource you choose, use it inventively

The 'liturgy' is literally 'the work of the people'. Certainly, organising Holy Week involves 'work'! But it is important that we try and ensure that the effort is directed to maximum effect.

Whatever resource is chosen for a particular moment of a particular day, we must be coherent and yet inventive in the way it is used.

Even though this book offers words to well-known hymn tunes, there is no need to expect everyone in the congregation to sing all of it from beginning to end. It is worth exploring how light and dark might be added to the singing of a text, and how its levels of meaning might be reinforced by sharing the song out, for example, between choir and people or between men and women – especially where there is a verse/chorus structure.

If songs are shared out in this way, it will help to avoid interrupting the flow of the celebration with unnecessary verbal instructions if the necessary rubrics are printed on the order of service or the hymn sheet. (See page 96 for the technical information which facilitates permission to reprint the copyright texts this book offers.)

Similarly, creative use of vocal and instrumental harmony can help make the message of a text more transparent thanks to the musical colour given to it. Again a simple example: the Liturgy of Light on Holy Saturday evening might be deliberately kept unaccompanied, instrumental accompaniment being introduced from the Liturgy of Initiation onwards, so that there is yet another 'passage', from *a cappella* to accompanied.

Silence is an important liturgical resource. Some of the symbols of the liturgy are obvious, others require time. Giving the congregation an intentional silence, the space and opportunity to reflect and so grasp some of these deeper symbolisms, will enable liturgies to mature.

Sometimes the solemnity of complete silence will be needed, notably for much of Good Friday.

However, not everyone is comfortable with absolute quiet, and some people will be more at home in a gentler silence, where they themselves are called upon to be still while enwrapped within appropriate background music. Sometimes, at the end of a song, it is good to allow a complete verse of the accompaniment (with variations, if practicable) so that people have the opportunity to go back over the phrases in the text that spoke to them. Where a song has a particularly concentrated text, one might insert musical interludes, so that one verse has had a chance to speak to people and reach their minds before their mouths are filled with the next!

Finally, good liturgy presumes good planning, which is to say *co-operative* planning. If a song is worth singing, it is because it contributes something to the celebrations, and it should be only natural that some of this finds its way into what the celebrant says, either as part of the address or monitions, or even as part of the sermon. This is a long-standing tradition in the church: Paul's letters often quote what clearly must have been hymns and liturgical texts. Indeed, what serves as the Gospel acclamation for Palm Sunday and for Good Friday is in fact the restoration to song form of part of a hymn that Paul quotes in his letter to the Philippians (cf. Phil 2:6-11).

Palm Sunday

FROM 'HOSANNA!' TO 'CRUCIFY HIM!'

1. What . . .

Those who have had to prepare the Palm Sunday liturgy will probably share our feeling of paradox, of being pulled in two different directions. On the one hand, there is the festive procession with its 'Hosannas'; on the other hand, the Gospel is the proclamation of the passion according to one of the synoptic accounts.

In part, this is because what were originally two distinct celebrations have been combined.

The Procession of Palms

This is one of the ceremonies borrowed from Jerusalem. There, of course, they had the advantage of being able to follow the route taken by Jesus and his disciples. We know from a fourth-century diary kept by a Spanish pilgrim called Etheria (or Egeria) that it was on the Sunday afternoon that the people gathered with the bishop at the Mount of Olives, went in procession first to the church of the Ascension, then down the hill, across the valley and up into Jerusalem, singing, 'Blessed is he who comes in the name of the Lord'. They processed slowly, on foot, and at a pace to suit the slowest. It was evening before everyone reached the basilica where the ceremony finished with night prayer and a special blessing.

Pilgrims took the idea back home, and a seventh-century book shows that the procession was known in Spain by then and probably earlier. The seventh century Celtic Bobbio Missal has a blessing of palms, and the procession was certainly well developed in ninth-century France. In AD 818 Bishop Theodulph of Orleans was exiled by King Louis to Angers. While there, he wrote a song, describing the palm procession in Angers: how the people from all the parishes gathered and made their way to the cathedral for Mass. The latter part of the song lists the parishes, but the first part was more general. Indeed, it became one of the standard songs for the procession in the West: *Gloria laus et honor tibi sit* (All glory, laud and honour).

Rome – notoriously conservative in adopting liturgical practices from elsewhere – does not have an official procession until the twelfth century, which is not to say that people were not instinctively celebrating it there earlier. There is an intriguing note in one of the liturgical books used by the monks at the Lateran: 'We don't have time to sing the *Gloria laus* because we need to have mass finished by the time the Pope arrives'!

The Proclamation of the Passion

The history of the eucharist of Palm Sunday is far simpler to recount. By the mid-fifth century we know for certain that at Rome the readings were Philippians 2 and the passion according to Saint Matthew. Pope Saint Leo (440-461) quotes the first reading in full (in Sermon 72); and it is clear from his other sermons that he preached on the passion according to Matthew – but in two stages, beginning on the Sunday and then taking it up again on the Wednesday.

We know, too, that in North Africa it was traditional to proclaim Matthew's account of the passion. Indeed, so traditional was it that when Saint Augustine (354-430, Bishop of Hippo from 395) tried to change the Gospel and use the passion according to one of the other synoptic evangelists, the people complained so much that he had to abandon the idea!

So we have today two solidly traditional elements: the procession and the passion. But how are we to make sense of them? Are they simply two different rites, with different origins, which somehow have become stuck together? Does today's feast expect us to switch suddenly from the exuberant joy of greeting Christ with 'Hosanna!' to the sombre condemnation 'Crucify him!'?

Not at all. If these two rites have grown together, it is because they *belong* together, because they are complementary:

- 'Hosanna . . . Blessed is he who comes in the name of the Lord' we sing in the procession.
  'Hosanna!' which means literally 'Mercy, Lord!' or 'Save us, Lord!'
  'Blessed is he who comes . . .' is an explicit welcoming of Jesus as the Christ, the Messiah, who 'comes in the name of the Lord'.
- 'Christ was humbler yet, even to accepting death . . .' we hear proclaimed in the second reading and then we sing to greet the Passion.
  The way that the Lord offers the salvation we shout for in our 'Hosanna' is the way of the cross, for Jesus – and for us.

The Messiah that the Lord sends is the suffering servant (cf. first reading, Isaiah 50).

But the liturgy does not leave us dumped in the sadness of the tomb:

- notice how Isaiah ends on a hopeful upbeat 'The Lord comes to my help . . . I know I shall not be shamed' (v 7);
- the ancient Christian song that Paul quotes (Phil 2:6-11) does even better, because the first half of humiliation (vs 6-8) is outbalanced by a second half of even greater glorification (vs. 9-11).

By throwing us into these two contrasting but complementary themes, the church offers us the perfect entry into Holy Week and the celebration of the Paschal Mystery. The Paschal Mystery which is precisely about the paradoxical process of the greatest possible glorification at the cost of the greatest possible humiliation. Listen to the elegant way that *Lent, Holy Week and Easter* balances and resolves these contradictions:

> 'Dying, you destroyed our death.
> Rising, you restored our life.
> Lord Jesus, come in glory.'

On this day, more than any other, our singing of the 'Holy, holy' with its 'Hosanna' should take on special significance.

2. How . . .

Processional Song

Here is a deliberate development of the Paschal paradox, borrowing a whole range of scriptural images. Verse 4 begins with an idea borrowed from Saint Andrew of Crete, which would make an excellent pastoral instruction to our modern-day congregations:

> 'Come, let us run with him as he presses on to his passion. Let us imitate those who have gone out to meet him, not scattering olive branches or garments or palms in his path, but spreading ourselves before him as best we can . . . So may we welcome the Word as he comes; so may God who cannot be contained within any bounds be contained in us.'

What matters is not the palms: what matters is the procession, the fact that the people make a physical gesture, a symbol of commitment to follow Christ not just through the Holy Week which begins today, but in life as in liturgy.

ODE TO JOY 87 87 D

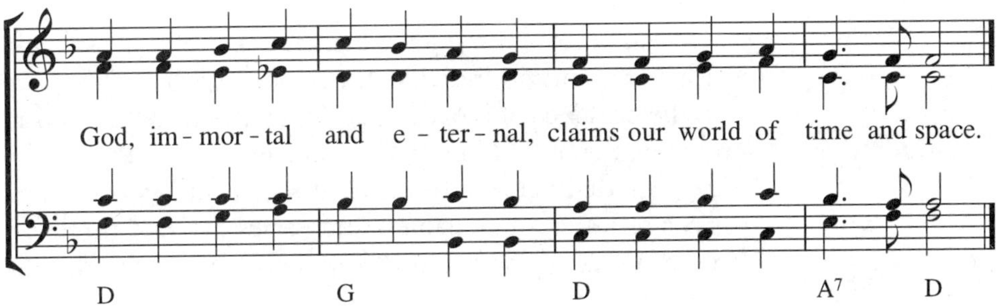

2
Though his glory comes through
torment,
and with thorns he will be crowned,
by his sacrificial dying
life abundant will be found.
Though to human eyes defeated,
he will triumph over pain:
love and joy will conquer hatred,
truth shall dance and peace shall reign.

3
Joyful songs of praise re-echo
and the very stones rejoice!
God in Christ exalts the humble,
gives the silent poor a voice.
See, he comes to end oppression,
and the captive to release,
heal the sick, restore the outcast,
and declare the age of peace.

4
Let the branches strewn before him
be the lives we offer here,
all our hopes with his united
in the love that casts out fear.
Sing hosanna to the Saviour,
coming in the Father's name;
God of mercy, save your people,
truth and liberty proclaim.

5
Gospel grace and gospel judgment
turn our structures upside down!
Christ reveals the greater glory:
wooden throne and thorny crown.
Priest and politician taunt him
and the fickle crowd deride,
yet, through tender confrontation,
God in Christ is glorified.

6
'Every valley, rise to meet him!
Mountains, level to a plain!'
Patriarchs and prophets greet him,
heaven and earth take up the strain!
All the world shall see his glory,
now in mortal flesh revealed,
when the poor are held of value
and the broken lives are healed.

Text: Michael Forster (b. 1946)
Music: Ludwig van Beethoven (1770-1827) arr. Christopher Tambling

Responsorial Psalm: Psalm 69

There can be no doubting the literary genre of this psalm: it is a lament, and an individual, personal lament at that. In fact, the presence of two distinct rhythms betrays that this is probably a combination of two laments. In the extract for today, the first verse is from the first lament (with the key themes of water and enemies) and verses two and three are from the second lament (the key theme being the devout person who suffers out of zeal for God).

In the Hebrew tradition it would be unthinkable to end a psalm in misery, so that even this psalm ends in hopeful praise (not quoted in the lectionary): sure that God will hear the cry of the afflicted, the psalmist sings, 'I will praise the name of God with song'. This is why we have added the fourth verse [in parentheses].

This psalm (together with psalm 22) is the most quoted by the New Testament, where it is imagined on the lips of Jesus as the exemplary suffering of an innocent person who relies on God for ultimate deliverance.

MELITA 88 88 88 (Eternal Father, strong to save)

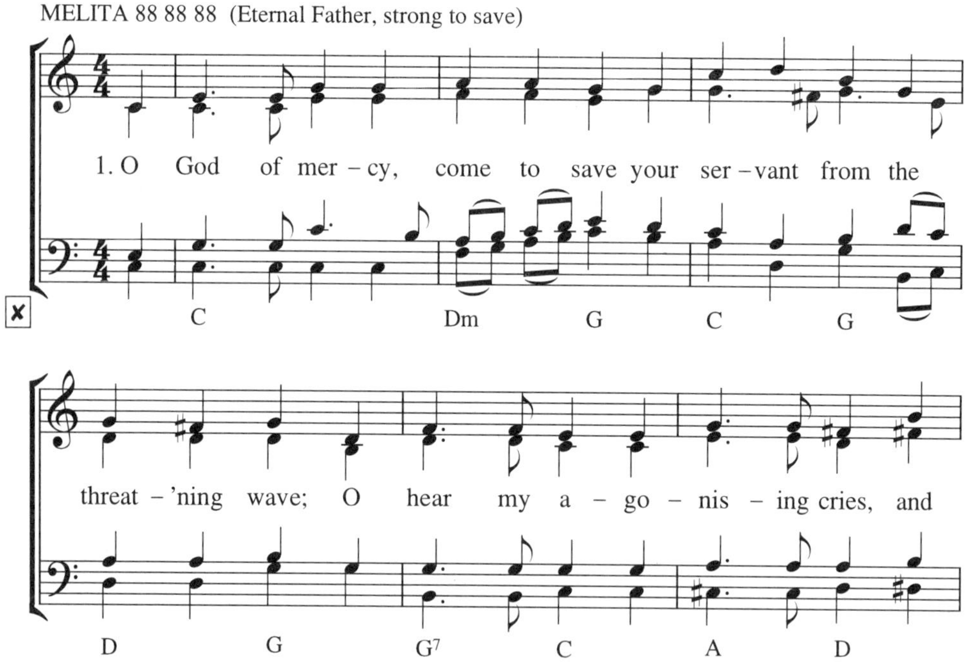

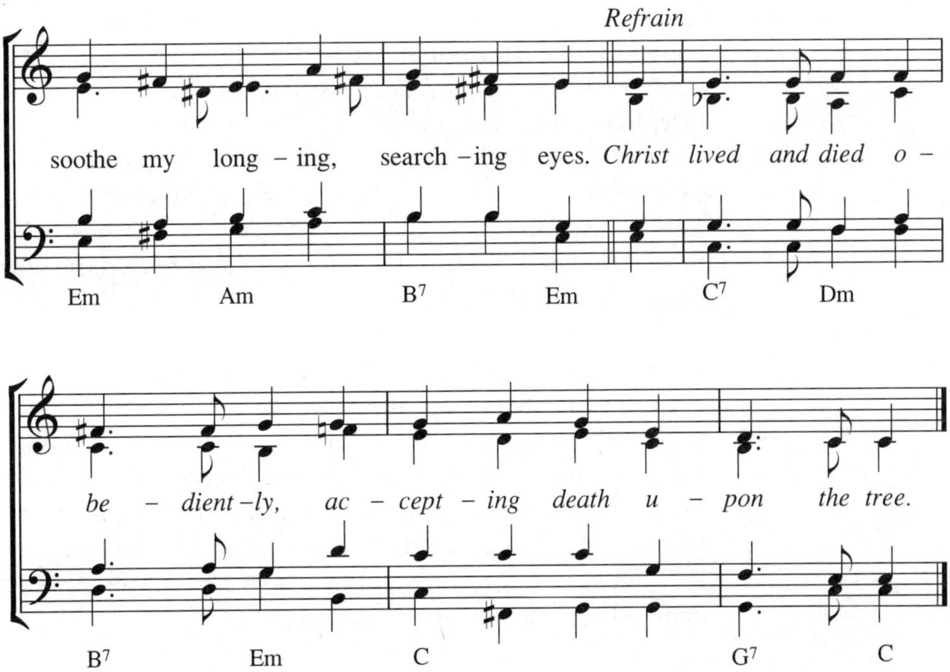

2
For you, O God, I suffer shame,
my loved ones fear to speak my name;
the insults heaped on you I feel,
my spirit burns with holy zeal.

3
Disgrace and shame have born me down,
and no compassion can be found;
no consolation will be mine,
but poisoned bread and bitter wine.

4
(Although beset by scorn and pain,
my God will lift me up again.
let every fainting heart be strong,
and praise the name of God in song.)

Text: Michael Forster (b. 1946)
Music: John Bacchus Dykes (1823-1876)

Gospel Acclamation: Philippians 2:6-11 (8-9)

Singing this is appropriate at several different levels. First and foremost, it respects the origin of the text, one of Christianity's earliest songs.

Secondly, to have it in metre and verse respects the poetic expression found in the original Greek. The Greek has only two sentences, which fall symmetrically into two sets of three strophes, hence our two sets of three verses. In the first three, Christ is the subject; in the second, it is God.

Thirdly, and not least, singing allows people the time to savour the magnificent theological content of the song.

Liturgy planners must make a pastoral judgment: whether to have Philippians 2:6-11 as a conventional second reading, followed by verses three and four below; or whether the psychological space given to the words by singing them might not help them be better appreciated. In the latter case it can either be read first and then repeated in full in song, or simply proclaimed in full in song.

SAINT CLEMENT 98 98 (The day thou gavest, Lord, is ended)

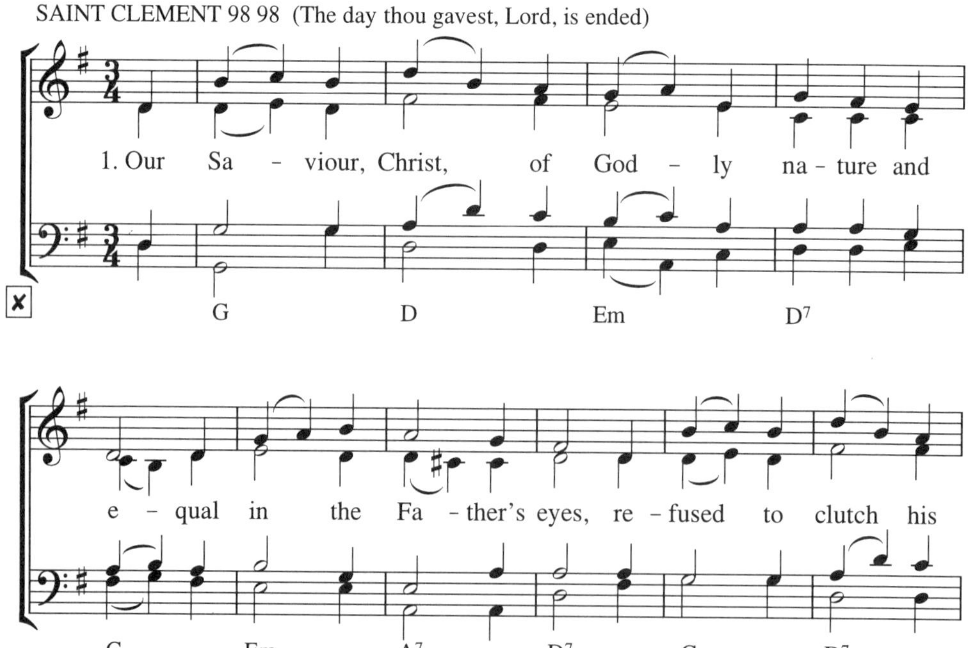

2
Of all his heav'nly glory emptied,
his very self he freely gave,
to clothe himself in human nature
and wear the mantle of a slave.

3
Immortal God for us made mortal,
the God-breathed Word drew human breath,
then gave up even that to save us,
obedient to the very death.

4
From death to life did God exalt him,
to heaven's joy and earth's acclaim;
on him, and him alone, bestowing
the Name above all other names:

5
That at the glorious name of Jesus
all nations shall acclaim his worth,
and every knee shall bow before him
above, below and on the earth.

6
Let every tongue in earth and heaven
proclaim that Jesus Christ is Lord,
who shows the glory of the Father,
our God for evermore adored.

Text: Michael Forster (b. 1946)
Music: Clement Cotterill Scholefield (1839-1904)

Responding to the Proclamation of the Passion

Whichever of the passages recommended in *Lent, Holy Week and Easter* is used, there is no doubt that the proclamation of the Passion has more impact when it is read in a dialogue form, which helps express the inherent drama. Because the text is so long, many parishes try and involve the community by giving them the crowd's parts. Unfortunately, this is the negative 'Crucify him!'

We propose here a positive alternative: to pause at appropriate moments, where there is a natural break in the rhythm of the passion narrative, and let the people make a prayerful response with the acclamations.

Matthew 26:14-29 *Mark 14:1-25* *Luke 22:14-38*

EVENTIDE 10 10 10 10 (Abide with me)

Matthew 26:30-56 *Mark 14:26-52* *Luke 22:39-53*

Christ, Lord of love, what treachery is this?
See how your friend betrays you with a kiss!
Change by your love all those who share his claim,
all who call hatred holy in your name.

Matthew 26:57-75 *Mark 14:53-72* *Luke 22:54-65*

Christ, by your friends in daily life denied,
bruised by the fall which follows sinful pride,
you, only you, can pardon and restore,
reach out your wounded hand to us once more.

Matthew 27:1-31 *Mark 15:1-15* *Luke 22:66-23:25*

Christ, Priest and Victim, this is now your hour,
victim of priests' and princes' lust for pow'r;
help us destroy the gods of pow'r and pride,
and stand with you among the crucified.

Matthew 27:32-50 *Mark 15:16-39*

Christ, who has shared your people's darkest fears,
Father who knows bereavement's bitter tears,
Spirit of love, with healing in your breath,
hold and unite us at the time of death.

Luke 23:26-46

Father and Spirit of the dying Son,
still undivided, Three for ever One,
grant at life's end that, trusting in your grace,
we may surrender to your love's embrace.

Text: Michael Forster (b. 1946)
Music: William Henry Monk (1823-1889)

The 'Hosanna' of the Eucharistic Prayer (Sanctus)

Earlier, in the section teasing out the meaning of this feast (page 19), we suggested 'Today, more than any other, our singing of the "Holy, holy" with its "Hosanna" should take on special significance'.

Here is a simple way to establish an intuitive connection between the 'Holy, holy' of the Eucharistic Prayer and the acclamations of the procession song: the following verses, to the same tune, have been constructed:

- around the traditional key words of the *Sanctus* (the repeated 'Holy', 'power', 'might', 'glory', 'the Lord's name', and, of course, 'Hosanna')
- to follow on from the preface to echo the Philippians reading ('humbly for our glory came')
- to express explicitly the eucharist as Christ's offering (cf. first reading, 'suffering' and 'thanksgiving').

ODE TO JOY 87 87 D

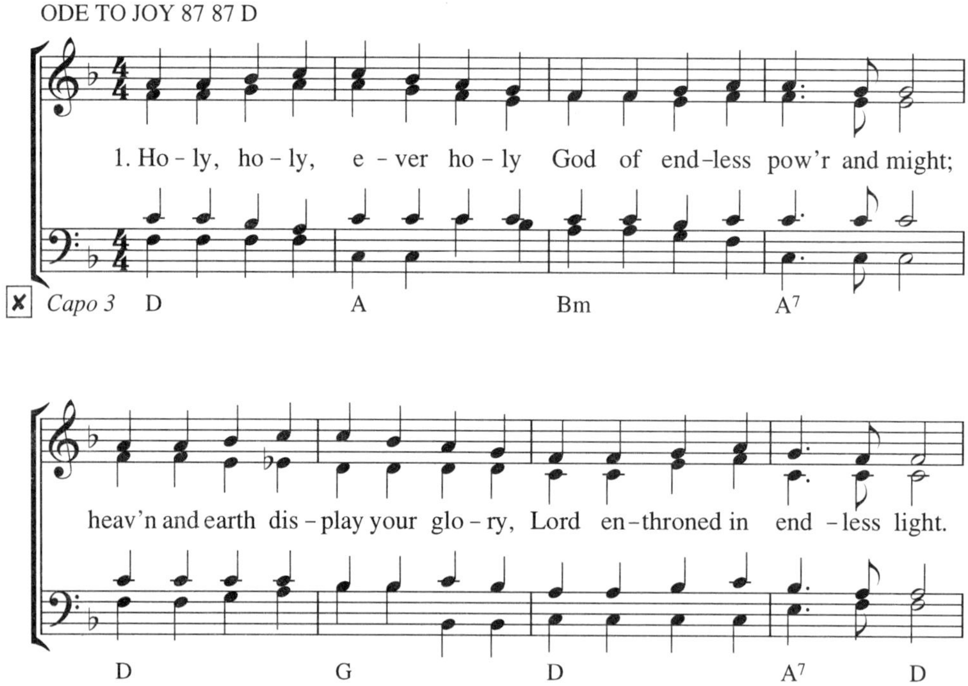

2
Blessèd is the coming Saviour,
sent in God his Father's name,
he whose flesh and blood are offered
sinful people to reclaim.
So we join our glad hosannas,
raise our voices to the height:
'Holy, holy, ever holy
God of endless pow'r and might!'

Text: Michael Forster (b. 1946)
Music: Ludwig van Beethoven (1770-1827) arr. Christopher Tambling

At the Breaking of the Bread (Agnus Dei)

To underline that it is the one, unique Paschal Mystery which we celebrate in every eucharist, and in which we are invited to share through communion in the broken bread, here is an *Agnus Dei* for the whole of Holy Week, but with a central verse special to today, which picks up the key notion of Christ coming to offer mercy and peace as Son of David; as Messiah, but as a Messiah who is to suffer.

REPTON 86 88 6 (Dear Lord and Father of mankind)

2
O Lamb of God, how silently
for slaughter you prepare.
Great Son of David, set us free
from mortal greed and vanity,
O hear our humble prayer,
O hear our humble prayer.

3
O Lamb of God, our lives restore,
our guilty souls release.
Into our lives your Spirit pour,
and let us live for evermore
in perfect heav'nly peace,
in perfect heav'nly peace.

Text: Michael Forster (b. 1946)
Music: Hubert Parry (1848-1918)

Maundy Thursday

'Do This, in Memory of Me'

1. What . . .

By comparison with Friday and Saturday, Thursday seems to offer a fairly conventional eucharistic celebration. When we look at how this day has been celebrated throughout history, however, we discover it is one of the richest of the church's liturgical days. No less than three distinct Masses, each with a very different purpose, have marked this day. Traditionally, Maundy Thursday was the occasion for the celebration of:

- the Mass for the Reconciliation of Penitents
- the Mass of Chrism
- the evening mass of the Lord's Supper.

Even though parishes celebrate only the last of these, knowing what these celebrations were and why they were associated with this day helps clarify which aspect of the Paschal Mystery it is that deserves our attention at this time.

Mass for the Reconciliation of Penitents

In the early church, the sacrament of penance was seen as 'a second baptism'; one of the earliest descriptions speaks of 'this baptism of tears'. The actual celebration of the sacrament was therefore structured parallel to baptism:

- Baptism was celebrated only once in a lifetime, as a public ceremony in front of the whole community, and after years of long and careful preparation; so, too, the sacrament of reconciliation: only once, in a public ceremony, and with a long period of preparation which was the time of doing penance.
- During their time of preparation the candidates for baptism had a special place in the church building and were only allowed to attend the Liturgy of the Word; so too, the penitents, those preparing for the sacrament of penance.
- Only the bishop administered baptism; so too, only the bishop presided over the granting of pardon.
- Baptism was celebrated only at the Paschal Vigil, followed immediately by confirmation and then, for the first time, the now-baptised candidates were allowed to stay on for the celebration of the eucharist and to receive communion. In order that the penitents could take their full and

proper part in the Easter Vigil, they had to be reconciled before the Vigil. This could not happen on Good Friday, because Good Friday was an a-liturgical day – no sacraments were celebrated (except in cases of danger of death). Which brings us to the Thursday.

So on Thursday morning there was a Mass at which the penitents, having fulfilled their penance (which lasted years, depending on the seriousness of their sins), and so having convinced the community that they were ready to be received back, were reconciled and granted solemn absolution by their bishop.

Mass of Chrism

As we have just observed, the Easter Vigil was normally the only occasion when new Christians received baptism and were confirmed. For both baptism and confirmation, oils are needed. These oils needed to be ready both in the physical sense that they had to be made up and in the spiritual sense of being consecrated, made holy.

With exactly the same sacramental logic as for the Mass of Reconciliation, the nearest appropriate day before Saturday is the Thursday: so, at midday, there was a special Mass, during which the oil of catechumens (for the pre-baptismal exorcism anointings) and the oil for the sick were blessed; and the oil of chrism was mixed and consecrated.

This solemn consecration then was reserved to the minister of baptism, in other words, the bishop. It is still today reserved to the bishop as a symbol of his pastoral responsibility for all the baptised in his diocese.

In many dioceses, there is a special Holy Week eucharist, presided over by the bishop, when clergy from the parishes bring their oils for consecration. This service may include the rite of the renewal of commitment to priestly service when all the priests of the diocese gather round their bishop and together they recommit themselves to their ordained priesthood, to the service of the priestly people of God.

The Evening Thanksgiving for the Eucharist

Again it is thanks to the fourth-century Spanish pilgrim whom we already met in the previous chapter, called Etheria or Egeria, that we have the first knowledge of an evening celebration of the eucharist on this Thursday. It was held in what is now the Paternoster Church on the Mount of Olives, the people going out afterwards to visit the Garden of Gethsemane.

Is this not strange? That for something as central as the memorial of the Last Supper, we have to wait four centuries?

The answer shows how much attitudes to liturgy have changed. Of course the early church celebrated the memorial of the Lord's Supper – but they did it Sunday by Sunday. The church and its liturgy were not about commemorating historical events, but about celebrating *mysteries*. Far more than remembering the historical past, the liturgy of the early church was understood as a foretaste of the banquet of the Kingdom of God. It is only because the people of Jerusalem had places with a historical link to Jesus' founding celebration that – as a special extra – they celebrated this evening mass.

We know that in sixth-century Rome there was a celebration at dusk, but again we can safely presume it was an 'extra' because it had no Liturgy of the Word. It is not until the eighth century that we have a mention of the readings that are now associated with this evening celebration. Quite naturally, they were: 1 Corinthians 11, which is the oldest extant account of the Lord's Supper (dating back to AD 57); and John 13: 'Jesus got up from table . . . and began to wash the disciples' feet'. But by the ninth century, we hear no more about an evening mass at Rome.

Lent, Holy Week and Easter restores the rite of the washing of the feet, to be celebrated after the Gospel. The oldest mention of this rite in Rome is from the seventh century, with the Pope washing his servants' feet. The tradition was still alive in the fifteenth century, though by now it was 12 subdeacons' feet that were to be washed. It was then, however, a full rite with both feet being washed, but by the nineteenth century it had been reduced to a symbolic rinsing of one foot. Elsewhere, it was understood as a baptismal rite: in Milan at the time of Ambrose (374-397) it took place during the Easter Vigil: the newly baptised had their feet washed after they emerged from the font.

2. How . . .

It is the three readings that offer the key to the meaning of this evening celebration. Exodus 12 declaring it is to be a day of *remembrance*, Paul takes up this theme, expressing it as *memorial* while adding that this memorial is not a mental exercise but an action: '**Do** this *as a memorial of me*'. And in case we miss the point, Paul has Christ say it in full twice, once for the bread and once for the cup. In the Gospel from John 13, the 'Do this' is expanded to become 'I have given you an example so that you may *copy what I have done to you*'.

However, a *memorial* of what? And we have to *do* what?

Those familiar with the Roman Missal may know that this is the only day of the year for which it offers specific advice on the content of the homily. It says that three things are being celebrated in the evening mass of the Lord's Supper:

- the institution of the eucharist
- the institution of the ministry of the priesthood
- the great commandment of love

In the Anglican tradition, the emphasis is on the first and last: thanksgiving for the institution of the Lord's Supper, and love expressed as the servanthood of all believers.

If we concentrate on love, the other elements in the list fall automatically into context:

- the eucharist is the promise of Christ's ultimate expression of love (and not a vain promise, for what he *says* tonight he *does* tomorrow)
- the ministry of the priesthood is the guarantee that Christ's own love will be passed on from generation to generation, kept alive in the life of the church

What is important about the eucharist and about the priesthood is that they are sacraments of Christ's love, making it real, present and effective, here and now.

It is the love of Christ that we are called to *remember*: It is the love of Christ that we are commanded in '*Do* this'. All that the church is and does, makes sense only in as much as it makes present and active the love of Christ. And when we say 'All that the church does', we are speaking primarily of the sacraments, the *raison d'être* of the church, which we have seen all have their place today. They have their natural place today because Christ is inaugurating the 'new and eternal covenant' of which these sacraments are the signs. Just as the old covenant was marked by a Law, so is the new covenant marked, proved, guaranteed by the new and greatest commandment of love.

Listen to what we pray for in the Collect for Maundy Thursday in *Lent, Holy Week and Easter*:

'God our Father,
you have invited us to *share* in the supper
which your only Son gave to his church . . .
May he . . . unite us in his *love* . . .'

Tonight's liturgy celebrates Christ's and – we claim in that prayer – *our* sharing of life and love. Until we have done that sharing of life and love – 'Do this' – our liturgy, no matter how splendid, how well sung, will remain superficial. Like

Christ, we must pass from saying it in celebration to doing it in life.

There are two particularly 'English' traditions which are inspired by this fundamental idea that what Christ asks us to 'Do in memory of him' is to express his love in the way we live our lives.

The first concerns the title given to this day. In other languages, it is merely 'Holy Thursday'; in English it is 'Maundy Thursday'. 'Maundy' is a corruption of the Latin word *mandatum*, which means 'command' or 'commandment'. '*Mandatum novum do vobis* – I give you a new command' (John 13:34). In other words this day has perceptively been named after its most central feature: the giving of the new covenant, with the new command which is the command to love as Christ loves.

There is also the tradition of 'Maundy money': nowadays this is a highly symbolic offering of money to the poor, because it is specially minted coins which are given by the reigning monarch to certain specially designated recipients. Again though, behind the ritualisation, we need to see the instinctive perception that Christ's utter selflessness is the model for the way we should behave.

Here is a simple, but well-founded idea that any parish of any denomination could adopt. Would it not be good if the message of the day so moved people that they were more generous to the poor today than any other day? Perhaps here is a non-liturgical, or more exactly a para-liturgical, way we could develop how we mark this day: by making it the focal moment of the parish's outreach to the poor. Obviously, the work of providing for the poor should go on throughout the year, but the more that this routine work can be linked to today's *mandatum*, the more Christian – in the truest sense – will be our offering, our work for the poor.

That is the real sense in which 'liturgy' is the 'work of the people': it is the task, the responsibility that Christ has entrusted to us, the 'work' through which his life and love can continue to be shared until it reaches its fulfilment in the coming of the kingdom. But with the work, the task, the responsibility, comes his grace, the empowerment of the Spirit. Here is the paradox of right and duty, of task and privilege, the paradox of the Paschal Mystery, which we dare to celebrate because Christ has commanded, 'Do this in memory of me'.

Responsorial Psalm: Psalm 116

A thanksgiving psalm, whose relevance will be grasped by everyone, as long as the words are clear enough! The allusions in this psalm led it to be one of those used in the Jewish Passover celebrations. An added appropriateness, then, because we can imagine this very psalm on the lips of Jesus and his disciples during their Last Supper.

This version lends itself to twofold treatment. Either a cantor or the choir could sing the verses, and the people sing the responsorial line.

Alternatively, everyone could be invited to sing all of it. In this case, the final lines could be adapted to suggest a progression in keeping with the central meaning of today's celebration:

Verse 1 The blessing-cup joins us in the *blood* of the Lord.
Verse 2 The blessing-cup joins us in the *life* of the Lord.
Verse 3 The blessing-cup joins us in the *love* of the Lord.

SLANE 10 11 11 12 (Lord of all hopefulness)

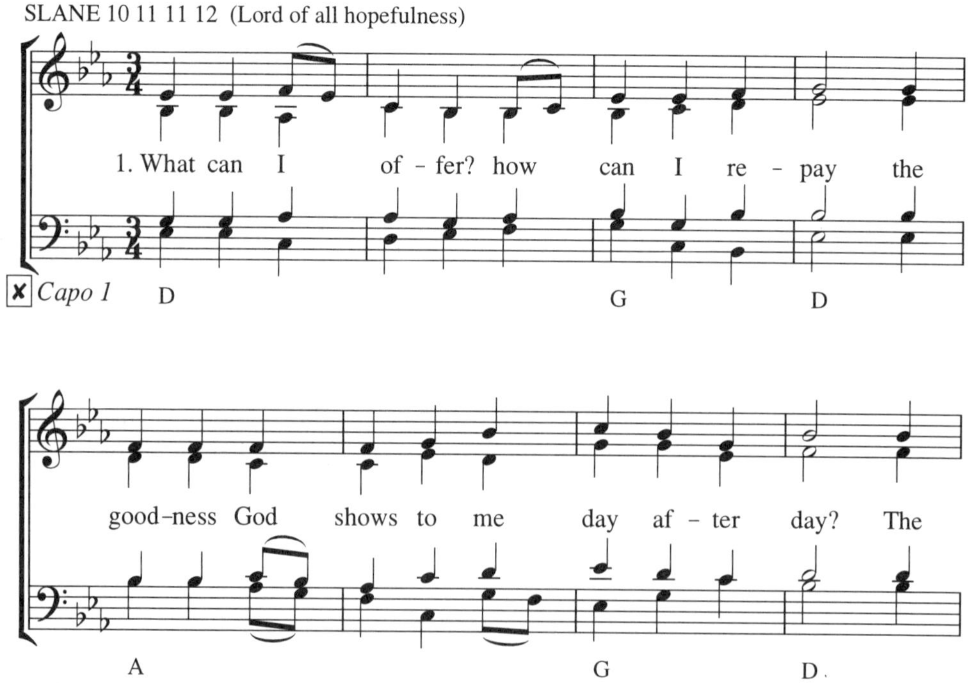

2
Grievous to God is the death of his own,
whose hairs he has counted, whose griefs he has known.
Lord, I am your servant, redeemed and restored,
The blessing-cup joins us in the blood of the Lord.

3
Now let our lives and our worship proclaim
thanksgiving to God, as we call on his name.
Our vows we shall honour with common accord,
The blessing-cup joins us in the blood of the Lord.

Text: Michael Forster (b. 1946)
Music: traditional Irish Melody arr. Colin Hand

Gospel Acclamation: John 13:34

Verse 3 of the hymn *Jesus, the King divine* on pages 40-41 may be used.

Song for the Washing of the Feet

The washing of the feet is a rite which is meant to have visual impact. It would not make sense, then, to oblige the people to have their noses glued to a hymn sheet! That is why, although the tune is well known to everyone, it is presented here in a verse/response structure: by giving the people the response to sing, at least during the verses they would be free to observe the rite, and let it speak to them, backed up by the words they hear sung and the response they sing themselves.

LOVE UNKNOWN 66 66 44 44 (My song is love unknown)

2
Low at our feet he kneels,
our Saviour and our Lord!
The love which Christ reveals
is more than earth affords!
We crush our pride,
accept with grace,
then take our place
at Jesus' side.

3
This new command I give:
to love as I love you,
and by the way you live
to show that love is true.
If this you do,
the world will see
you are in me,
and I in you.

4
Faith, hope and love, these three
eternally remain,
forever flowing free,
and never spent in vain.
As from above
God's graces flow,
his people know
the best is love.

Text: Michael Forster (b. 1946)
Music: John Ireland (1879-1962)

Song for the Collection of the Offerings for the Poor

The tradition of the monarch's distribution of Maundy money symbolises the church's calling to offer gifts to the poor. Although this is not (unfortunately) specifically stated in the ASB text, the church presumes that, if we have understood what it is we are celebrating tonight, we will express our sharing not just symbolically but in a real and physical way by such gifts. There is a magnificent text, traditionally associated with this day, which leaves us in no doubt about the self-sacrifice to which this feast commits us: it is the *Ubi caritas.*

This is a song where the use of different voices would help give expression to the central theme of the celebration: the presence of Christ in love, underlined by the constant response, 'There God is found'.

Here is an example:

Choir men or male solo Where the love of Christ unites us,
People *there God is found.*
Choir women or female solo Where we meet as love invites us,
People *there God is found.*
Choir Let us come with jubilation
to the God of our salvation;
love enlivens all creation:
People *there God is found.*

AR HYD Y NOS 84 84 88 84 (All through the night)

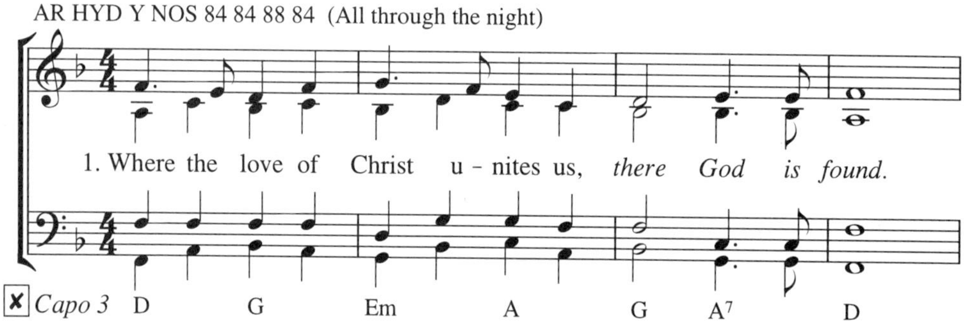

2
Where we meet without division,
there God is found,
free from anger and derision,
there God is found.
Let all bitter feuds be ended,
strife resolved and foes befriended,
pride and fear by love transcended:
there God is found.

3
Where the blessèd live for ever,
there God is found;
bonds of love no pain can sever,
there God is found.
Christ in glory, we implore you,
let us with the saints adore you,
love resplendent flows before you;
there God is found.

Text: Michael Forster (b. 1946)
Music: traditional Welsh melody arr. Colin Hand

At the Breaking of the Bread (Agnus Dei)

We propose the *Agnus Dei* as for the other eucharistic celebrations of Holy Week, but with a central verse which focuses on the symbolism of tonight's celebration; both the bread and wine, and Christ's expression of service in the washing of the feet.

REPTON 86 88 6 (Dear Lord and Father of mankind)

2
O Lamb of God, our living bread,
and joy's free flowing wine,
our humble servant, yet our Head,
by your own life our souls are fed,
in holy Word and Sign,
in holy Word and Sign.

3
O Lamb of God, our lives restore,
our guilty souls release.
Into our lives your Spirit pour,
and let us live for evermore
in perfect heav'nly peace,
in perfect hean'nly peace.

Text: Michael Forster (b. 1946)
Music: Hubert Parry (1845-1918)

Song for the Watch

Lent, Holy Week and Easter suggests: 'If the Watch is to be kept, there may be a procession and a hymn or psalm may be sung.' Originally, the procession had a functional purpose, but one which underlines the essential unity of Thursday's and Friday's celebration. By tradition, some parishes observe Good Friday as an a-liturgical day. Yet, although no eucharist can be celebrated, it is recommended that Communion be shared – but it is the Communion consecrated at the Thursday evening eucharist. So it is that Communion is taken in procession to the place of reservation. Even if the sacrament is not to be reserved, a procession to a different place for the Watch can highlight for us, yet again, that what Christ *says* on the Thursday he *does* on the Friday.

The last verse of this song reminds us how Christ himself left the place of the supper, and retired to the Garden of Gethsemane, to pray with an earnestness which Saint Luke describes very graphically: 'his sweat fell to the ground like great drops of blood' (Luke 22:44). Traditionally, we too are invited to spend some time in prayer, before the altar of repose if applicable.

PASSION CHORALE 76 76 D (O sacred head ill-usèd)

2 The voice of Jesus calls us
to share his humble reign,
his baptism of sorrow,
his cup of hope and pain.
The signs of blood and water
still draw us to his side,
where flowing scarlet glory
drowns all our mortal pride.

3 We hear the words of Jesus,
'I give myself to you,'
and then his dread commandment,
'This also you must do.'
Like bread, let us be broken,
like wine, let us be poured,
that we may be for others
the body of the Lord.

4 'O let this cup pass from me,
yet may your will prevail.'
Though weak may be the body,
the spirit will not fail.
So may the church, though broken
by wounds of sin and shame,
enlivened by Christ's spirit,
bring glory to his name.

Text: Michael Forster (b. 1946)
Music: Hans Leo Hassler (1564-1612) harmonised by J. S. Bach

Good Friday

'It is Accomplished'

1. What . . .

Today's celebration is quite remarkable. A sense of the importance of this day has led Christians throughout the centuries to celebrate it with dignity and sobriety, but with an enormous respect for the tradition that was handed on to them. So we who stand on the threshold of the twenty-first century celebrate a liturgy whose basic form was familiar to our Christian predecessors in the early second century and all whose elements were in place before the year 400.

In summary we have:

- a classic liturgy of the word whose structure (readings-homily-intercessions) matches what Justin describes taking place in Rome in AD 150
- a rite of proclamation of the cross which took shape in fourth-century Jerusalem
- a simple rite of ante-communion, which conforms to the practice of the early church (when Mass was celebrated only on Sundays).

The Liturgy of the Word

There was a stage, very early on, when the only way this Friday was marked by Christians was by the solemn fast that commemorated the forty hours that Christ was in the tomb. The Saturday night was the celebration of Christ's Paschal Mystery, celebrating in one single vigil his death, resurrection and glorification. When Good Friday did come to have a Liturgy of the Word, it was by stretching part of the Vigil forward; it borrowed some of the Vigil's readings. These were Hosea 6, Exodus 12 and the passion according to John.

Now, in the lectionary, the passion according to John has been retained. The other readings include: Isaiah 52-53 (the classic 'song of the suffering servant'); Hebrews 4-5 (Christ's passion and death making him the one and only true priest).

The first extant versions of the Good Friday prayers date from around the fourth or fifth century – almost certainly revisions of earlier third-century forms. The shape of the prayer points to its antiquity, dating back to a time before the church's concept of itself as a priestly people was eroded by clericalisation and the increasing appropriation of the liturgy by the ordained ministers. Note how marvellously the structure expresses the church in action. Everyone is involved, all the baptised, but each in their own different and complementary way, together fulfilling their 'priestly' role. A deacon announces the intention; all kneel to make silent, individual prayer for that intention; but as a sign that the concluding prayer is not just the prayer of the celebrant bishop, all stand in the priestly posture. It is truly the Prayer of *all* the Faithful.

The solemn intercessions of Good Friday survived because of the esteem in which they were held by successive generations of Christians. Perhaps because they instinctively perceived that the mystery we celebrate on Good Friday gives meaning to all Christian prayer, but especially to the highest form of liturgical prayer of supplication – the Prayer of the Faithful.

It is by the mystery of the cross, the altar on which the New Lamb's blood is shed, that we are made a new and priestly people, born out of the water and blood from the side of Christ to continue his priestly work. It is in triumph as High Priest on the cross that Christ becomes the unique true mediator between God and humankind, interceding to the Father of the world. So too this priestly people, born of the cross, continues that priestly work, intercedes to the Father for the church and for the world that the church has to serve. It is only through the merits which Christ by his death has won that we are able, in Christ's name, to petition the Father.

The Proclamation of the Cross

For the origins of this rite we are back in fourth-century Jerusalem. In her diary, our Spanish pilgrim Etheria explains at length how the rite unfolded in what was Constantine's basilica, recently built (dedicated in AD 335) on the site of Golgotha and the garden Tomb. The Emperor's mother, Saint Helen, is said to have discovered the remains of the cross.

Gathered around the very site of the cross, with the very wood of the cross, what other way could the Christians of Jerusalem celebrate this day? Everyone, catechumens as well as faithful, came forward in procession to a table on which, laid out before the bishop, was the remnant of the cross. Etheria even notes the presence of two deacons, either side of the bishop, whose task it was to safeguard the relic, because it seems some over-enthusiastic pilgrims tried to get themselves a souvenir by sinking their teeth into it! From daybreak to midday the ritual lasted – presumably in silence, for Etheria makes no mention of either readings or songs.

Pilgrims like Etheria took back enthusiastic accounts of the liturgies they had experienced, and gradually we find the rite being imitated.

In seventh-century Rome, for example, we know that the Pope walked barefoot from the Lateran to the Church of the Holy Cross in procession, incensing a relic of the cross carried before him by a deacon. We know, too, that during this procession Psalm 118 was sung, with 'Behold the wood of the cross on which hung the Saviour of the world: come and worship' as an antiphon.

Imitation of this rite did not depend on having a relic of the cross. An eighth-century book describes this Friday succinctly as follows: 'After the general intercessions, everyone adores the cross, and receives communion.'

It is just about this time that we have the first evidence of a rite of unveiling (although this does not catch on in conservative Rome until the twelfth century). To make sense of this rite, we have to appreciate that the representation of Christ would have been one of him *in triumph* on the cross, as the Great High Priest. So, earlier in Holy Week, as the focus of the liturgy is the *passion* of Christ, this figure was hidden, to be revealed on Good Friday as the church celebrated the triumph of the cross. 'We should glory in the cross of our Lord Jesus Christ, for he is our salvation, our life and our resurrection; through him we are saved and made free' (Galatians 6:14).

It is in the twelfth century, too, that Rome first uses the Reproaches. The oldest extant trace of the first three verses is in a ninth-century French antiphonary, but they clearly are older, perhaps even as early as the seventh century. However, the style of the reproaches is distinctly Eastern. Jerusalem in the seventh century had a different text, but in very much the same style: images from Exodus challenging images from the New Testament.

The Ministry of the Sacrament

Whether the eucharist should be celebrated on Good Friday is, according to *Lent, Holy Week and Easter*, a 'vexed question'. Two quite different views are recognised, and the service pattern may be adapted to accommodate either. Whether or not the eucharist is *celebrated*, however, it is strongly recommended that it should be *received* (using elements consecrated on the Thursday) as a sacramental participation in the self-offering of Christ.

2. How . . .

An A-liturgical Day

We have already used this expression several times, to express a fundamental intuition of the church as to how this day should be marked.

If it is true that the sacraments are the celebration of the presence of Christ, it makes sense to abstain from the sacraments to mark this day when Christ accepts to be utterly absent in death.

An Imposing Silence

There is no entry song today. This is not an oversight, but a deliberate choice of silence.

The people should gather in silence. Will they realise it is an intended, deliberate silence? If it is liable to be filled with the hustle-bustle of people gathering together, it may be pastorally more useful to disguise this behind a discreet and appropriate piece of music which actually encourages people to be calm, hushed and reflective. However, this should be noticeably different from the usual entry voluntary, if such is the parish custom. This might be achieved by playing a piece of recorded music (for example: the slow movement from Mahler's Fifth Symphony; Albinoni's *Adagio for Organ and Strings*; Samuel Barber's *Adagio for Strings*).

In all events, any such background music needs to stop, clearly and purposefully, so that the entry of the ministers can take place in complete silence: a silence which should continue right through the prostration of the ministers (during which the people kneel in silent prayer) and be broken by the celebrant who alone stands to pray the Collect aloud.

Psalm 22

This is the psalm for today, and *Lent, Holy Week and Easter* recommends that it may be read, followed by a spoken antiphonal response. In metrical form, this response would be inordinately long, but an alternative might be to use the metricated version of Psalm 22 offered here.

As is fitting for today, this psalm is a combination of two moods, two literary genres: lament and thanksgiving. This psalm is used frequently in the Gospel passion narratives: Christ is the fulfilment, first in the suffering, but thereby also in thanksgiving. The greatest thanks we can offer is 'where your people gather round', that is, in the liturgy, to offer the thanksgiving of Christ himself. The words used by Christ on the cross become a refrain in this metrical version.

So that the response, the words used by Christ, take on an added weight, it may be good to treat this as a verse-chorus song: either a soloist or the choir sing the verse section, and all respond with the chorus.

PICARDY 87 87 87 (Let all mortal flesh keep silence)

2
Now the snarling rabble gather,
clamouring in spiteful tones.
See, my hands and feet are broken,
I can even count my bones.

3
See how they divide my clothing,
gambling for the coat I wore,
O my strength, make haste to help me,
Lord, abandon me no more.

4
I will sing your endless glory
where your people gather round:
'All God's people shout his praises,
let your songs of joy resound!'

Text: Michael Forster (b. 1946)
Music: traditional French melody arr. Christopher Tambling

Gospel Acclamation: Philippians 2:6-11 (8-9)

Please refer to page 24 for an explanation and setting of this text.

Responding to the proclamation of the Passion according to John

As for Passion Sunday, we offer prayerful sung responses which can be used at appropriate moments during the proclamation of the passion.

John 18:1-9

EVENTIDE 10 10 10 10 (Abide with me)

John 18:10-27

2
Christ, by your friends in daily life denied,
bruised by the fall which follows sinful pride,
you, only you, can pardon and restore,
reach out your wounded hand to us once more.

John 18:28-40

3
Truly '*bar-Abbas*', Christ the *Father's Son*,
sinless, you die for every guilty one:
call us to witness truth, and hear your voice,
justice and righteousness shall be our choice.

John 19:1-16

4
Christ, Priest and Victim, this is now your hour,
victim of priests' and princes' lust for power;
help us destroy the gods of pow'r and pride,
and stand with you among the crucified.

John 19:17-30

5
Christ, Son of Mary, Brother of us all,
give us the grace to answer to your call.
Grant us to live by faith, that, when we die,
your 'It is finished' is our final cry.

Text: Michael Forster (b. 1946)
Music: William Henry Monk (1823-1889)

Songs at the Proclamation of the Cross 1. The Reproaches

Here is a song written in the tradition of 'The Reproaches', where the saving intervention of God in the Old Testament, particularly in Exodus, is contrasted with the treatment meted out to Christ in his passion and death.

This Eastern literary song genre worked thanks to a double choir who 'threw' the contrasting phrases at each other. This simple technique can be copied in our modern-day celebrations by dividing the 'contrasts' between, for example, the voices of men and women. In all events, the song has been written with a constant chorus, so that the whole assembly can take an active part in this meditation on God's work of salvation throughout human history.

FINLANDIA 10 10 10 10 10 10 (Be still, my soul)

2
For forty years I was your constant guide,
I fed you with my manna from on high.
I led you out to live in hope and peace,
but you led out my only Son to die.

3
With cloud and fire I marked the desert way,
I heard your cries of rage and calmed your fear.
I opened up the sea and led you through,
but you have opened Christ with nail and spear.

4
When in distress you cried to me for food,
I sent you quails in answer to your call,
and saving water from the desert rock,
but to my Son you offered bitter gall.

5
I gave you joy when you were in despair,
with songs of hope, I set your hearts on fire;
crowned you with grace, the people of my choice,
but you have crowned my Christ with thorny briar.

6
When you were weak, exploited and oppressed,
I heard your cry and listened to your plea.
I raised you up to honour and renown,
but you have raised me on a shameful tree.

Text: Michael Forster (b. 1946)
Music: Jean Sibelius (1865-1957)

2. Song of the Cross

There is a tradition of acclaiming the cross as Christ's instrument of triumph by meditating in song on the scriptural typology of the role of wood in the hands of God in the history of salvation. There is, for example, the *Crux Fidelis*, with the verses:

Pange lingua, gloriosi lauream dertaminis
et super crucis trophœo dic triumphem nobilem . . .

which Ronald Knox translated as

Sing my tongue of warfare ended, of the Victor's laurelled crown;
let the cross, his trophy splendid, be the theme of high renown . . .

The song goes on to evoke the cross as the new Tree, undoing the harm that came from the tree in the Garden of Eden, as the new Noah's Ark.

There is also the late-sixth-century hymn by Venantius Fortunatus, *Vexilla Regis*, which can be found in most modern hymnals translated as 'The royal banners forward go' (J. M. Neale translation), or as 'Christ's banner guides us' (James Quinn S.J. translation). This concentrates on the image of the cross as 'the Tree'.

Modern hymn writers have used the same imagery: in the Stanbrook Abbey hymnal we find the metricated hymn 'O cross of Christ, immortal tree'; in a much more modern style, there is 'Wood hath hope' by John Foley of the Saint Louis Jesuits.

In this same long tradition, here is a celebration of the moments of salvation that God has effected by means of wood, seeing in them all the foreshadowing of the cross. The wealth of images, gleaned from Old and New Testament, is enclosed within an opening which explicitly expresses our thanks, and an ending where Christ reigns in triumph 'enthroned on wood . . .'.

AURELIA 76 76 D (The Church's one foundation)

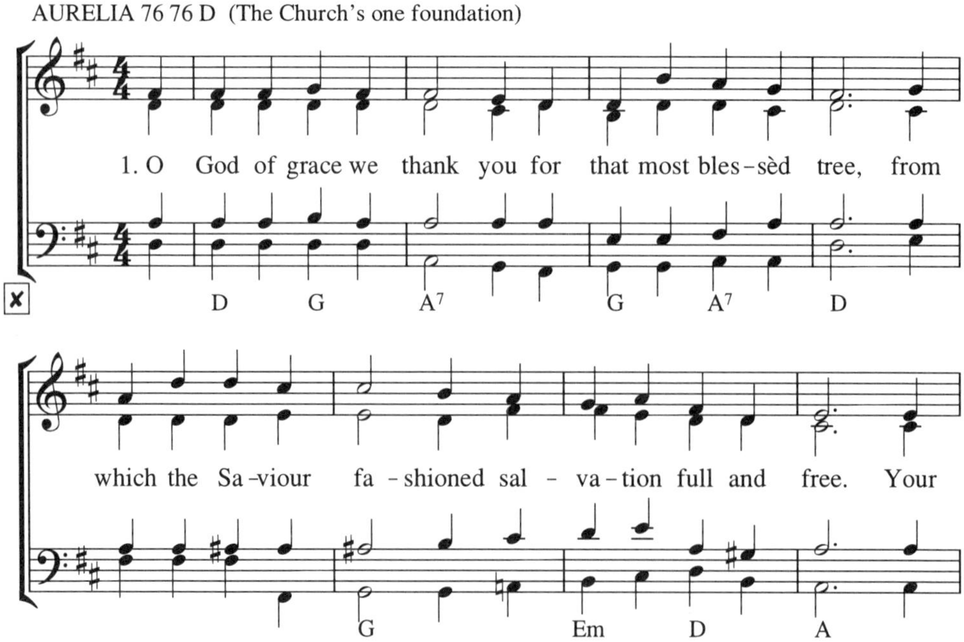

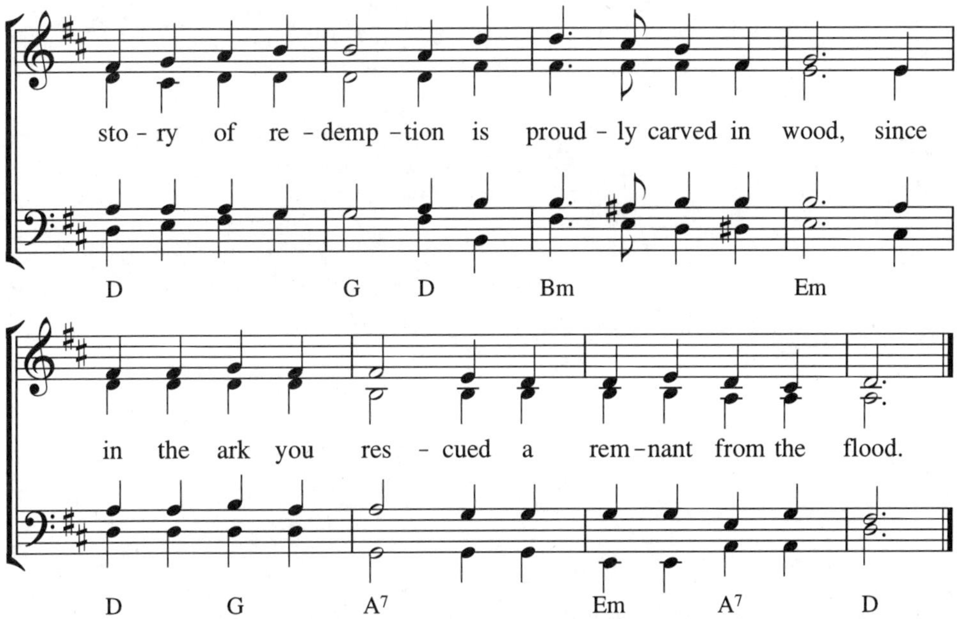

2 The bush that lit the desert –
'though burned, yet not consumed –
became the seed of promise
from which salvation bloomed.
The light of life eternal
still shines with hope and joy,
from him whom hell's inferno
could burn but not destroy.

3 The staff which Moses carried,
as shepherd of your choice,
is lifted high to rally
the sheep who know your voice.
From farthest bounds, you call us,
as people of the cross,
to find eternal value
in your most bitter loss.

4 Christ is the vine eternal,
producing wholesome fruit;
the rod that brings salvation,
the branch from Jesse's root.
In crib and crucifixion,
in boats upon the sea,
the Saviour's earthly journey
is shadowed by the tree.

5 This tree of life gives knowledge
of love that conquers all,
the fruits of goodness ripen,
and evil's strongholds fall.
It sprang from this creation
of which we all are made,
and where, by sign and symbol,
your purpose is displayed.

6 The log which, in the desert,
made bitter water sweet,
transforms the foulest hatred,
and renders hope complete;
for in its awesome presence
all earthly glory pales:
the Carpenter is reigning,
enthroned on wood and nails.

Text: Michael Forster (b. 1946)
Music: Samuel Sebastian Wesley (1810-1876)

Easter Vigil

'This is the Night . . .'

Our Greatest Feast

A progression through the liturgical ceremonies of Holy Week, well celebrated, should have built up a sense of anticipation, of longing, for tonight's liturgy. In this sense, the richness of the Easter Vigil should come as a fulfilment of the people's longing – and not as an extra long ceremony simply to be endured.

As was suggested in the introductory chapter, the way the whole liturgical year has been celebrated has hopefully been leading our congregations to this climactic night – since all the year's feast and celebrations take their meaning from the Paschal Mystery which is celebrated in a supreme way at the Easter Vigil.

Ideally, this ought to find natural expression in the Vigil being the best-attended of the year's celebrations. Perhaps we ought to be more explicitly conscious of this throughout the year, and use those moments which are particularly well attended to whet the people's liturgical appetite for the Easter Vigil.

For example, if Christmas is the 'busiest' Mass of the year, suggest, tactfully, that the genuine joy of celebrating the nativity of the Lord is to return to celebrate the real feast of his Lordship, the Easter Vigil.

If Ash Wednesday is the best attended liturgical occasion then again we might diplomatically offer the suggestion that there is infinitely more meaning in people having their forehead marked with ashes if they are also there at the Vigil to have the same forehead washed clean with the newly consecrated baptismal water.

The tradition of the church offers a truly magnificent collage of ritual, symbols, gestures and words. The Vigil is complex, but it is not complicated. A natural procession of rites should be allowed to wash over the people, so that by absorbing what they see, hear, smell and feel, the actual physical experience of the Vigil awakens a greater understanding of what the Paschal Mystery means.

This would be an onerous task, an awesome responsibility for liturgy planners, if they had to start from scratch! Instead, the church offers a fourfold but unified structure to enable us to lead our people through the liturgy into Christ's own Passover.

That is the key to this night, the constant underlying motif to all that is said and done: it is a *passover*, a *passage* from one state to another. The liturgy planners' task is to make these four *passages* as vivid as possible, so that the people feel they are caught up in the Passover they share with Christ.

1. What . . .

As proof of the Vigil's antiquity, we need look no further than when it begins. It begins at dusk; in other words, according to the Jewish tradition of counting the days, which run from dusk to dusk. We will hear this same time calculation expressed in the first of the Vigil readings when each day of creation is logged off as 'Evening came and morning came . . .'.

In other words, this is a celebration which dates back to apostolic times when Christians still celebrated within the structures of the Jewish faith. Beyond that, it is not just antiquity for antiquity's sake: is it not more uplifting, more optimistic if the day is calculated as beginning in darkness which then gives way to the second part in light?

It is this timing which led quite naturally to the development of the first of tonight's four liturgical sections.

The Vigil

Although that title is no longer specifically used in *Lent, Holy Week and Easter*, this element has played a vital role in shaping the liturgy as we now have it. Originally, having gathered at dusk, the Christians spent the night in listening to readings and in praying, until dawn. We have a description of what happened in Rome around AD 215 in what is known as the *Apostolic Tradition* of Hippolytus (incidentally, this same source provided the inspiration for our modern-day Eucharistic Prayer 3 of Rite A in the ASB). Hippolytus tells how the Christians spent the Saturday night 'in vigil, reading the scriptures and being instructed in them'.

An even older source gives us a clue as to what readings were used: a homily by Melito of Sardis, preached at a vigil in AD 166, spans the history of salvation beginning specifically with the first Passover of Exodus 12 and ending with Christ's death and resurrection.

We know that in second-century Rome they used Hosea 6 and Exodus 12, and what we would nowadays call the passion according to Saint John – except that they read it right through to the resurrection and beyond, to John 20:17 which includes a hint of the ascension.

Throughout history, various scripture texts came in and out of favour. The story of the flood, of Noah and the ark, used to be one of twelve readings used in Rome. If you are lucky enough to have pastoral circumstances where the assembly are ready and willing to keep vigil through the night until day, this is certainly an 'extra' reading to add to those the lectionary offers.

What is important, however, is to see the *purpose* underlying the scripture passages chosen, whatever they were, whatever they happen to be.

The use of the word 'recalling' echoes the great theme of Thursday, 'memorial'. As indeed it should, for the Thursday is the celebration of the Jewish Pesach or Passover, the ritual meal during which, still today, the Jews gather in families to remember 'this is the night God saves us'; to recall in particular the crossing of the sea and the escape from Egypt. A central feature of the Passover is *Haggadah*, 'remembering'.

As Christians, as inheritors of the promise made in word and deed to the first Chosen People, we take up their solemn tradition of remembering and proclaim, in the words of scripture, the successive *passages* through which God led us, his new people in Christ, to salvation.

We need to be sure, though, what the church means by 'recalling'. The church is not inviting us to imagine that we are back in time before Christ, and then work our way through the Old Testament. This is a typically 'historical' mind-set which is relatively modern, and very prevalent in the West. In our culture, then, 'recalling' often means thinking ourselves from the present into the past. What the liturgy invites us to do in 'recalling' is to pull the past, and even the future, into the present. We are called to celebrate what we are and what we might become. Events are the stuff of history, and we 'commemorate' them; mysteries are the stuff of liturgy which, by celebrating and making memory, we make actual. We are celebrating a passover, a redemptive process in which we are already caught up and which is working toward its complete fulfilment. As human beings, in a world of time, commemorating events may help us to recognise, be more alert to moments in that trans-historical process; but the 'recalling' that operates in the liturgy is the actualisation of the process itself, in us, here and now.

Knowing this underlying principle helps make sense of the patchwork of scriptural texts that today's lectionary spreads before us. A full list may be found in *Lent, Holy Week and Easter*, pages 240 ff, but the following give a good indication of the progression.

Genesis 1	the song of creation, celebrating the first *passover* from nothingness into being
Genesis 22	Isaac is *passed over* and saved from death
Exodus 14	the Israelites *pass* through the Red Sea *passover* from slavery to freedom
Isaiah 54	*passover* from rejection to re-acceptance
Isaiah 55	*passover* from want to plenty, from hunger to eating and drinking one's fill *passover* [from the existing covenant] into 'an everlasting covenant'
Baruch 3-4	passing from being enlightened ('wisdom') to living an enlightened life ('law') passover to light, reconciliation with God
Ezekiel 36	*passover* from exile back to the promised land from heart of stone to heart of flesh from defilement to purification
Romans 6	our *passover* [through baptism] into the death of Christ, so as to rise with him, and to live in Christ, in order to be with Christ for ever
Gospels	**Matthew 28:1-10 Mark 16:1-8 Luke 24:1-12** In this choice of readings from the synoptic gospels, each evangelist is allowed to present his account of the empty tomb. What they have in common is that none of them dares to account for, much less recount or describe, the resurrection. That is a mystery, which can only be celebrated, shared and lived.

The lectionary invites us to make a choice among these readings based on 'pastoral reasons', with the proviso that Exodus 14 must always be used. The 'How' section of this chapter (page 68 ff) offers additional comment on the readings which may help guide this decision.

There is one last important point of principle, which concerns the structure of the Liturgy of the Word. There is a regular pattern, whereby:

- we hear the reading proclaimed
- we respond to it in song (with another extract from scripture)
- we respond to it in prayer (through a brief moment of silent prayer, the collect said aloud on our behalf, and our assent in 'Amen').

In the way we celebrate, we must respect the unity of each section; let the psalm and the prayer, which have been designed in a very specific way to correspond to the reading, have their place, flowing on naturally from it. Our celebration of these three elements should flow naturally into one another with no sense of break between them. They are simply three modes of responding to the reading: by listening, by singing a response, and (enlivened by the reading) by praying. However, once the prayer is concluded (with a rousing 'Amen!') there *should* be the sense of a natural break, as our attention is directed to a different scripture text with its own emphasis, its own expression of *passover*.

The Liturgy of Light

This liturgy, as we now have it, is a combination of different cultural traditions: there is the Jewish and generally Eastern custom of lighting candles, to which has been added the Celtic tradition of the sacred bonfire.

This of course dates from a time when the Liturgy of Light was the opening liturgy, coming before the Liturgy of the Word (now designated 'The Vigil' and placed at the beginning). Therefore it was possible and appropriate to begin the celebration outside and process into the building. We attempt to highlight below some ways in which this custom heightened the experience of *passover* which is central to the Easter celebrations. It might well be worth considering reverting to this ancient custom and reordering the liturgy appropriately so that the Vigil precedes the Liturgy of Light. However, if it is preferred to stay with the more modern order, then the fire could simply be replaced by the candle.

The fire was part of the Celtic tradition, and used to mark the two greatest days in the Celtic calendar: the Celtic New Year (which was Christianised as All Saints' Day, by the way) and the Spring Festival. By the fifth century the fire had been adopted in Spain, and by the eighth century it was being used in Germany.

There is considerable evidence that testifies to the Christian Celts celebrating Easter at a time other than the rest of Western Christendom. Most liturgical commentators look for a Judæo-Christian explanation of this, whereas a pagan Celtic one may lie behind it. Let us imagine Easter being celebrated at the Spring equinox: what would the people be experiencing? This is the day when for the first time the light is equal to the darkness, and from now on will have the upper hand. What a magnificent liturgical and catechetical tool for enabling the people to understand that tonight Christ the Light overcomes the darkness of death and the spiritual darkness of sin. The Celtic bonfire is lit in defiance of the night, declaring boldly to the world of nature that we have the means to cast aside darkness.

If the liturgy is to say this, we must have a convincing bonfire! Since the Celts could manage it in the windswept conditions of fourth- to sixth-century Ireland, Western Scotland, etc., surely it is not beyond our capabilities, with all our modern sophisticated techniques, to organise a bonfire which confidently defies the night. Such a conflagration will have added symbolism as the people around it pass not just from darkness to light but from cold to warmth.

There is another feature of the bonfire which is not just practical but highly symbolic. If a real fire is used (rather than just a handful of charcoal lit in a brazier) it has to be *outside*. This is not accidental. Here is yet another way in which the Passover is made to come alive for us, since we are obliged to *pass* physically from outside to inside the building.

What effects this transition is a switch from the symbolism of the fire to that of the Paschal candle, lit from the sacred fire and preceding the people into the church where it will burn throughout Eastertide, and at all baptisms, as a reminder of the Passover which is celebrated and which takes effect tonight.

The paschal candle was being used by some churches in Rome (though not the papal liturgy) by the fourth century. We know this because Saint Jerome complains about some deacons who used the *Exsultet*, the sung proclamation which poetically heightened its symbolism, as a chance to show off their singing!

This proclamation has a very simple purpose: to put before us a range of scriptural references related to light and/or fire, and thereby help our appreciation of the Easter Christ as our Light.

The Liturgy of Initiation

Let us return to Hippolytus, and the *Apostolic Tradition*, which represents the liturgy in Rome in AD 215. After the night spent in vigil, as dawn comes up, the candidates are led to the place of baptism where the bishop prays over the waters. The candidates are stripped; they renounce Satan and are anointed with the oil of exorcism. Then naked, they descend into the water; there they are asked to profess their faith in God as Father, Son and Spirit, and with each affirmation they are immersed in the waters. As they come up after this triple immersion, they are anointed with what Hippolytus calls 'the oil of thanksgiving', dried, dressed in white and led back to the main body of the church. Now, in full view of the assembly, the bishop invokes the grace of the Holy Spirit upon them and their baptism is publicly sealed by the anointing with chrism. They exchange the kiss of peace and, for the first time, take their place in the assembly as members of 'the faithful'.

Beyond the general shape, there are elements of the rite which are in themselves very ancient. In particular, the prayer for the blessing of the baptismal water stretches back to the early church. It is constructed like a eucharist prayer: a section of praise, recalling God's saving intervention through water, which is followed by the prayer of consecration. The praise section bears witness to what constituted the Liturgy of the Word: in order to help convey that baptism is nothing less than our personal sharing in the redemptive passover God wills for all his people, the prayer was constructed to echo the scripture texts which would have been read, meditated and studied during the all-night vigil.

Hence we find a very clear reference to Genesis 1; there is an equally clear allusion to the flood, which although no longer included in our modern-day lectionary is explicitly mentioned in Isaiah 54; there is, of course, the recalling of Exodus 14 and the crossing of the Red Sea. The prayer also retains a key reference to John's symbolic testimony of water and blood flowing from Christ's side: as we have noted several times already, the original Gospel for this night was the passion, death and resurrection according to John.

The Liturgy of the Eucharist

If the sacraments of initiation offer a personal focus on our sharing in Christ's redemptive Passover, that focus now shifts to our sharing as a community in the Paschal Mystery. Gathered as Christ's body (including the newly baptised) the assembly as church makes Christ present, and active, here and now.

2. How . . .

VIGIL
Genesis 1 – Song of Creation

The first 'week' of creation comes from a tradition of liturgical song. As we read over the text, we cannot fail to notice the repeated choruses, responses: 'And so it was'; 'God saw that it was good'; but especially the main chorus which marks off the days: 'Evening came and morning came . . .'

There are musical settings which respect the literary genre of this responsorial poem, by offering sung versions of the responses.

Here is an alternative, simpler suggestion, which (in keeping with the aim of this book) is within the scope of any community. The original nature of the text is still respected; however, the focus here is the recurring 'God saw that it was good' response.

Our idea here is to put on the lips of our congregations a response to the 'goodness' of God. With the choruses offered below, each time that the narrator tells us that 'God saw it was good', we are able to echo that with an expression of our thanksgiving for a particular feature of the God-given creation.

Our focus, as we sing this, is not just 'backwards' to the mythical first week. There is a sense of the present, because we believe that here and now God sustains creation in being.

Our focus is also a *paschal* one; as Easter people we proclaim 'what the Word has brought about', seeing the resurrection as the new 'first' day, and ourselves as sons and daughters of the new 'time', in which God intends us to 'take delight'.

Responding in this way within the reading, day by day, would clearly eliminate the need for a responsorial psalm. Nonetheless, on page 70 we offer a metrical version of Psalm 33 for those who wish to use it.

Genesis 1:1-4a

SANDYS SM (Teach me, my God and King)

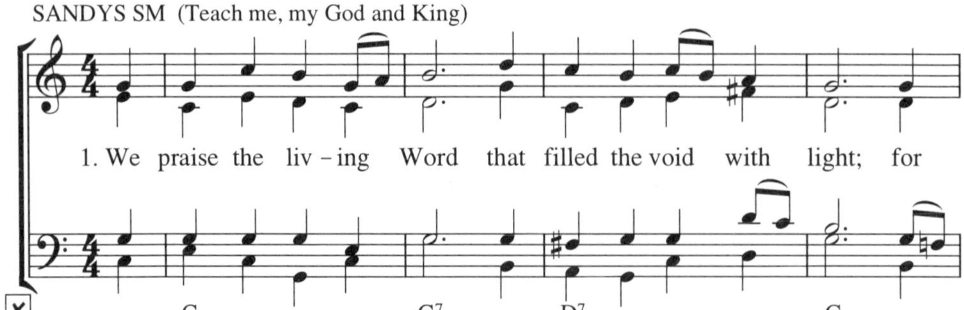

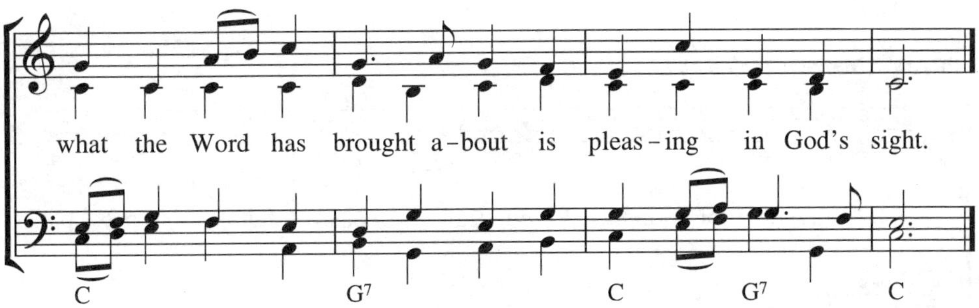

Genesis 1:4b-10

2
Great ocean depths, resound!
Give thanks, you mountain heights;
for what the Word has brought about
is pleasing in God's sight.

Genesis 1:11-12

3
In everything that grows,
let earth and heav'n delight;
for what the Word has brought about
is pleasing in God's sight.

Genesis 1:13-18

4
Praise God for each new day,
and every restful night;
for what the Word has brought about
is pleasing in God's sight.

Genesis 1:19-21

5
Give thanks to God for life,
in ocean or in flight;
for what the Word has brought about
is pleasing in God's sight.

Genesis 1:22-25

6
Let every creature praise
the God of pow'r and might;
for what the Word has brought about
is pleasing in God's sight.

Genesis 1:26-31

7
Let all the human race,
throughout the earth, unite;
for what the Word has brought about
is perfect in God's sight.

Genesis 1:31b-2:3

8
In worship and in rest
God's people take delight,
for what the Word has brought about
is holy in God's sight.

Text: Michael Forster (b. 1946)
Music: traditional English carol from William Sandys' *Christmas Carols* (1833)

Psalm 33:1-9 (following Genesis 1)

PRAISE, MY SOUL 87 87 87

2
For the words of God are faithful,
and his actions show his worth,
loving righteousness and justice,
pouring love upon the earth.

3
By his word he made the heavens,
by his breath, the stars in space;
gathered all the formless waters
in his treasure trove of grace.

4
Let the whole creation fear him,
and all people stand in awe:
when he spoke, it was accomplished;
his command was swift and sure.

Text: Michael Forster (b. 1946)
Music: John Goss (1800-1880)

Psalm 16 (following Genesis 22)

Following the very dramatic account of 'the binding of Isaac' (as it is traditionally known by Hebrew scholars) the liturgy seems to be putting this psalm of being rescued from death on the lips of Isaac – but Isaac as a 'type' or promise of Christ himself. The apostles, in their preaching, applied this psalm to Christ's conquest of death (see Acts 2:25-31 and 13:34-37).

SAINT PATRICK'S BREASTPLATE 88 88 D

2
So shall my heart and soul rejoice,
as on your strength I rest and stay;
you will not leave my soul to die,
nor let your loved one know decay.

3
Lord, where you lead me, life is found,
and in your presence joy and peace;
at your right hand, your people find
hope and delight that never cease.

Text: Michael Forster (b. 1946)
Music: traditional Irish melodies arr. Charles Villiers Stanford (1852-1924)

Exodus 15 (following Exodus 14)

First, an extremely practical point. It is very important to notice the way the reading flows into the canticle. There should be no break between the proclaimed word and the outburst of triumphant song.

The way the song pictures God as a military victor is a sign of the text's antiquity: the primitive Semitic people considered military activity as sacred.

Some scholars date the song (or at least the most ancient parts of it) to the thirteenth century BC, which would make this scripture's oldest sacred song. It is easy to imagine how the immensity and the importance of the event it commemorates certainly helped its survival throughout history, so that the song in itself becomes a mirror of what it recounts and what it commands: 'Come, sing to God'!

Here is a metrical version of the canticle, to a tune which respects the primitive vigour of the text.

WOODLANDS 10 10 10 10 (Tell out, my soul)

2
Come, sing to God, for glorious is his name,
to all the world his saving works proclaim.
God is our strength, his glory has been shown:
the power of evil he has overthrown.

3
Come, sing to God in this his triumph hour;
his strong right arm has shown his glorious power.
God is our strength, his vict'ry is complete:
oppression's forces languish in defeat.

4
Come, sing to God, the God of truth and grace,
within whose sanctuary we take our place.
God is our strength, we worship and adore!
The Lord our God shall reign for evermore.

Text: Michael Forster (b. 1946)
Music: Walter Greatorex (1877-1949)

Psalm 30 (following Isaiah 54)

Isaiah 54 is a post-exilic text (from what is known as Deutero-Isaiah) which starts from the covenant image of husband-wife; despite disastrous moments in this relationship (the author compares the exile with the flood) the power that God showed in creation will be surpassed by his redemptive power ('though the hills be shaken . . . my covenant with you shall never be shaken'). The precious stones that are to adorn the promised new city are precisely those that reflect the blue and the green of the original creation.

Beginning as an individual expression of thanksgiving to God for having been saved from death, Psalm 30 soon turns outwards to invite others to join in the praise. It might help the congregation understand the psalm better if the way it is sung reflects this: a soloist could sing verse 1, but all sing verse 2. Verse 3 returns to a personal reflection, so again it could be proclaimed by a soloist.

ODE TO JOY 87 87 D

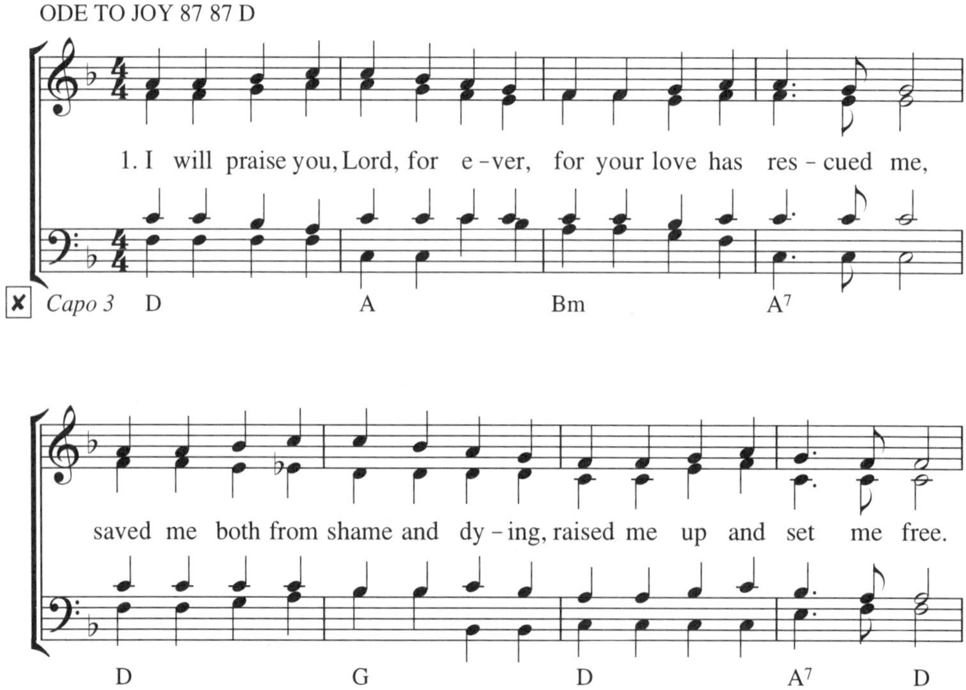

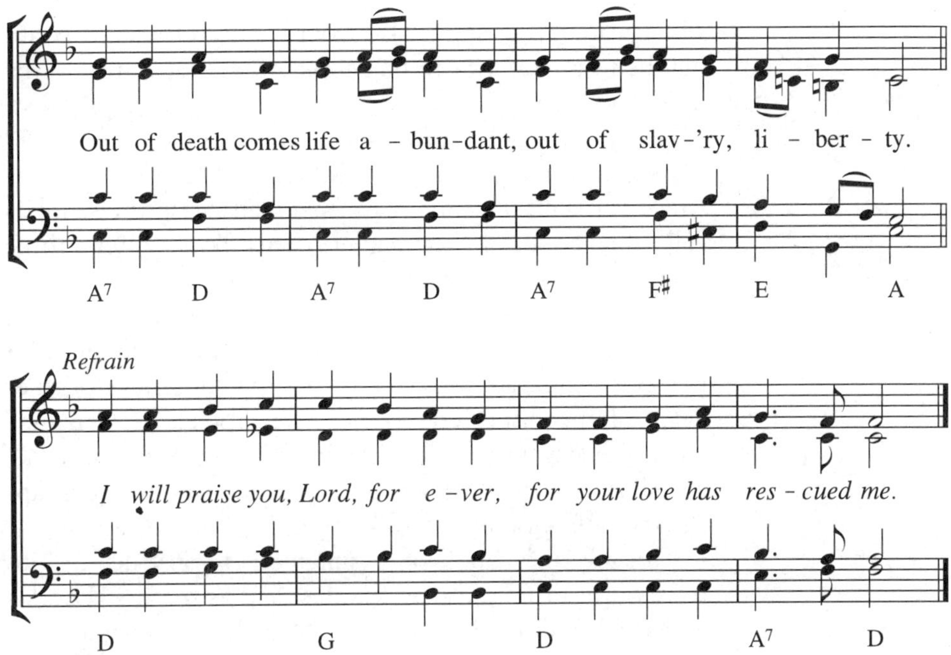

2
Sing to God, all you who love him,
thank his great and holy name,
for his wrath is always fleeting,
but his love remains the same.
Those who spend the night in weeping
soon his dawn of joy will see.

3
God has listened and had pity,
coming to his people's aid;
grief and tears give way to dancing
where his glory is displayed.
Songs of joy and glad thanksgiving,
I will sing eternally:

Text: Michael Forster (b. 1946)
Music: from the *Paderborn Gesangbuch* (1765)

Isaiah 12 (following Isaiah 55)

The Isaiah 55 reading is also from Deutero-Isaiah, describing the feast that awaits the people when they return to the new Jerusalem.

Isaiah 12, which serves as a response, is over a hundred years older, and it is in fact the Canticle of Thanksgiving which is the closing climax to what many scripture scholars call 'the Book of Emmanuel'. This book offers three promises: firstly, the coming of the 'Prince of Peace (8:23-9:6); secondly, the vision of the restoration of creation/Eden under the rule of 'Emmanuel' (11:1-9), and thirdly (in what is a post-exilic addition, 11:10-16) the gathering together again of the dispersed people. The 'Book of Emmanuel' ends with this tiny chapter 12, which is a song, far more like a psalm than a piece of prophetic writing, and may perhaps be a combination of two older songs.

The way the 'Book of Emmanuel' is constructed is to trace out a promised new Exodus: just as the first Exodus ended with an exuberant hymn of praise, so now an outburst of thanksgiving greets the announcement of the new Exodus to the new Jerusalem.

All these promises the church sees fulfilled in Christ.

SAGINA 88 88 88 extended (And can it be)

2
God is the Lord, my strength, my song,
the one my heart and soul adore.
Gladly, this water we shall draw
from wells of wholeness evermore.

3
Let us give thanks and praise to God,
and call upon his holy name:
tell of his works to all the world,
his glorious majesty proclaim.

Text: Michael Forster (b. 1946)
Music: Thomas Campbell (1825-1876)

Psalm 19 (following Baruch 3-4)

This Baruch reading is rarely chosen to be proclaimed during the Vigil. Certainly its style makes it less immediately accessible to people. However, this is a reading whose double focus on 'light' and 'law' will come alive if you have candidates for initiation at the Vigil. 'Enlightenment' used to be one of the names given to baptism in the early church: this corresponds exactly to the double focus of the text. On the one hand, in baptism, *we* are enlightened; but it is in order that we live *lives* that are enlightened, i.e. following God's laws.

If this double focus has been well expressed in the reading, the psalm will be a perfect response – a song welcoming the light the Lord offers which is nothing other than wisdom, i.e. living wisely, enlightened by his law.

Notice that the underlying mood is one of delight at having been given the Law. It is not an onerous task: on the contrary, it is enlightenment, worth more than anything the world can offer. Let it be our aim that the way we sing the psalm expresses this joy and appreciation!

CRÜGER 76 76 D (Hail to the Lord's anointed)

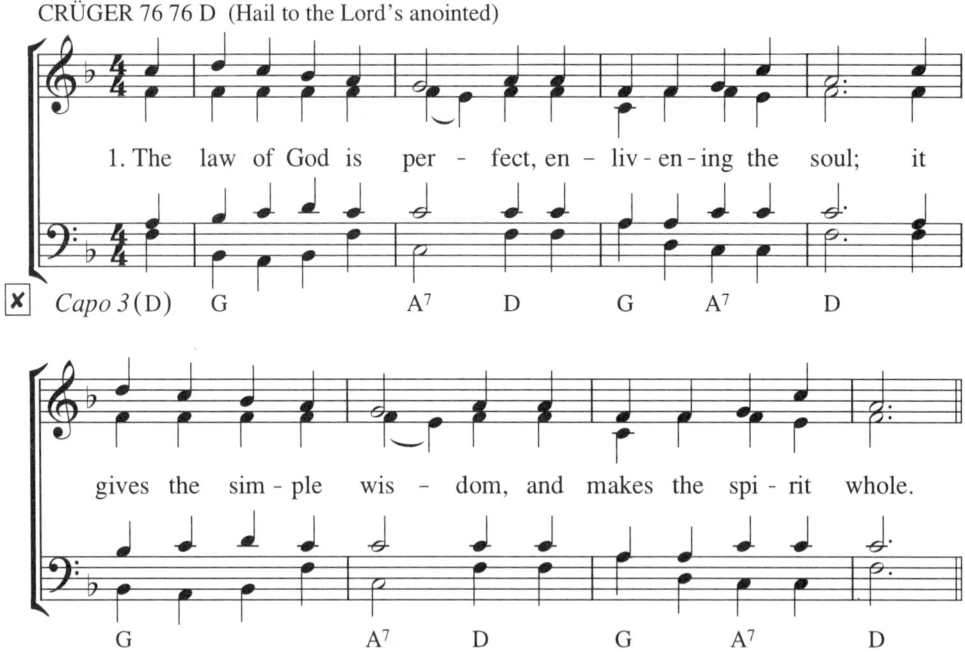

2
By knowledge of his statutes,
our hearts with gladness rise;
his crystal clear commandment
gives light to faithful eyes.

3
The fear of God is holy,
and ever will abide;
his laws are just and truthful,
our never failing guide.

4
Above all things, we treasure
your true and wise decree,
much more than gold and silver,
or honey from the bee.

Text: Michael Forster (b. 1946)
Music: from a melody in Johann Crüger's *Gesangbuch*
adapted by William Henry Monk (1823-1889)

Psalms 41 and 42 (following Ezekiel 36)

Ezekiel offers us a remarkable text, which works towards a climactic promise of a new creation which will surpass everything that Genesis 1 offered, and this despite the mess humankind has made of both the first creation ('defilement') and the first covenant with God ('idolatry'). It contains the specific promise of the Spirit which, in the universalist spin that the prophet Joel will give it, is quoted in the church's first ever sermon (Pentecost: Acts 2:16ff).

Although only Psalm 42 is specified at this point, it is worth considering the use of both 41 and 42, restoring them to their original form of a single poem. It is a song of longing, and on our lips becomes a prayer for the fulfilment in us of the prophecy of Ezekiel.

An encouraging aside for liturgy planners: note how a longing to be in the presence of God is fed by the memory of magnificent liturgies in the temple: may our efforts to offer a rich and meaningful liturgy inspire similar longings in all who take part.

HYFRYDOL 87 87 D (Alleluia, sing to Jesus)

2
All these things I will remember,
as my heart and soul I pour,
how I joined the crowd, rejoicing
in your temple to adore.

3
Send your light and truth before me,
let them be my only guide;
lead me to your holy mountain,
to the place where you abide.

4
I will come before your altar,
you the God whom I adore;
sing to you my glad thanksgiving,
God, my God for evermore.

LITURGY OF LIGHT
Song for the Procession of the Easter Candle

Here is a metrical hymn, which follows exactly the centuries-old tradition of the *Exsultet*, evoking scriptural images related to fire and/or light. There is an alternative version on page 230 of *Lent, Holy Week and Easter* and an alternative metrical version on page 287 of *Lent, Holy Week and Easter.*

DARWALL'S 148TH 66 66 44 44 (Ye holy angels bright)

2
Rejoice O shining earth,
in glorious hope reborn,
and praise the Light who wrought
the first creation's dawn.
Redeemed and free,
in Christ we rise,
and darkness dies
eternally.

3
Rejoice O Mother church;
on you the Saviour shines:
then let the vaults resound
with peace and joy divine!
His truth proclaim,
and loud and long,
in glorious song,
exalt his name.

4
The people who have walked
in terror through the night,
from shades of death released,
have seen a glorious light.
God's word is sure,
and he will bless
with righteousness
the humble poor.

5
O God of hope and love,
who lit the desert way,
and led from slav'ry's night
to liberation's day:
still go before,
till we rejoice,
with heart and voice,
on Canaan's shore.

6
We light these gentle flames
to be our pledge and sign:
we share the risen life
of Christ, the light divine.
Throughout the earth,
oppression's night
shall flee the light
of human worth.

7
Arise O Morning Star,
O Sun who never sets,
and raise these humble flames
to greater glory yet.
Let all adore,
in glorious strains,
the Christ who reigns
for evermore.

Text: Michael Forster (b. 1946)
Music: John Darwall (1731-1789)
harmonised by William Henry Monk (1823-1889)

Psalm 118 (following Romans 6)

The moment for images is past: we are struck by the directness with which Paul proclaims, ‘We went into the tomb with Christ . . .’. This homily on baptism works by playing off a whole series of comparisons (death/life, slavery/freedom, etc.), the most fundamental of which is that, through baptism, what happened to Christ happens to us. *Baptism is our Passover with Christ.*

Remember the exuberance with which Holy Week began, with the welcoming of Christ as Messiah in the procession of palms? This psalm is the song which accompanied that welcome (‘Hosanna. Blessed is he . . .’ is from this psalm), which Christians sing tonight, recognising now the full and true nature of Christ’s Lordship.

But it is not only Christ’s victory, for Paul has just told us we share in it fully. So it is not only Christ who proclaims defiantly in the Psalm ‘I shall not die’, but it can be each one of us. By singing this, and by living as if we mean it, we obey Paul’s exhortation ‘consider yourselves as alive for God in Christ Jesus’.

GOD REST YOU MERRY 86 86 86 and Refrain

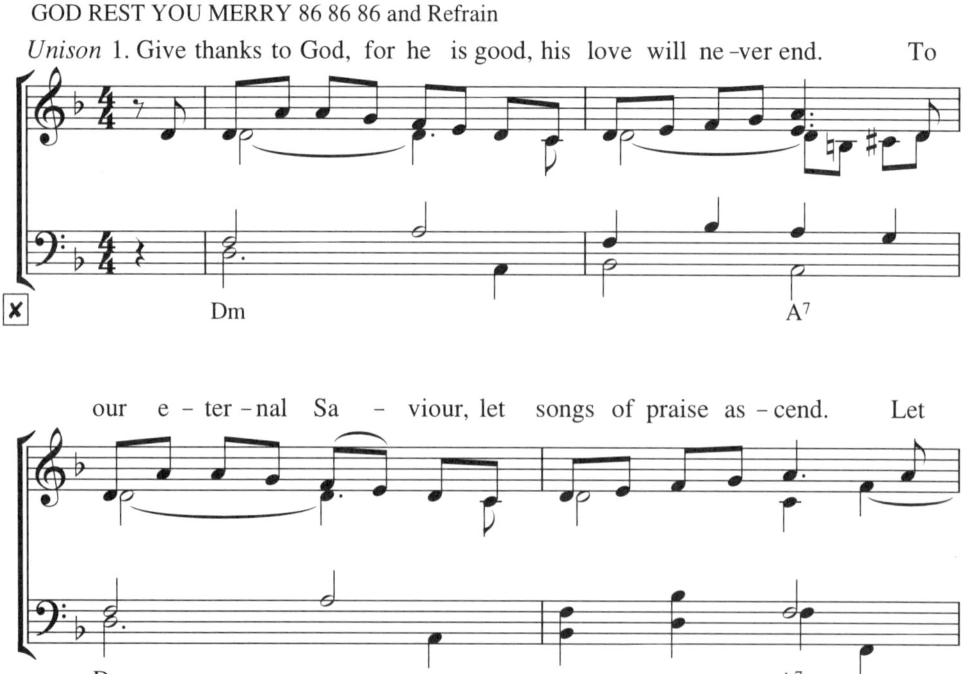

2
The Lord has triumphed gloriously,
his hand has raised me high.
Now I shall tell his wonders,
and never shall I die.
Let all his people sing with joy,
'His hand has raised me high.'

3
The stone the builders cast aside
is now the cornerstone,
a work by which God's glory
and faithfulness are shown.
Let all his people sing with joy,
'He is our cornerstone.'

Text: Michael Forster (b. 1946)
Music: traditional English melody arr. Adrian Vernon Fish

LITURGY OF INITIATION

Lent, Holy Week and Easter gives the simplest of indications: baptism and/or confirmation may take place.

In the early tradition of the church (and as continued in today's Roman Missal, for example), the first part of the initiation ritual was to bless the water (see page 67).

We offer here a hymn which is based on the thanksgiving part of the very ancient prayer of blessing, which is in fact a meditation on the images of water as a sign of redemption, as conveyed by the Vigil readings.

Blessing of the Baptismal Water

BATTLE HYMN 15 15 15 6 and Refrain (Glory, glory hallelujah)

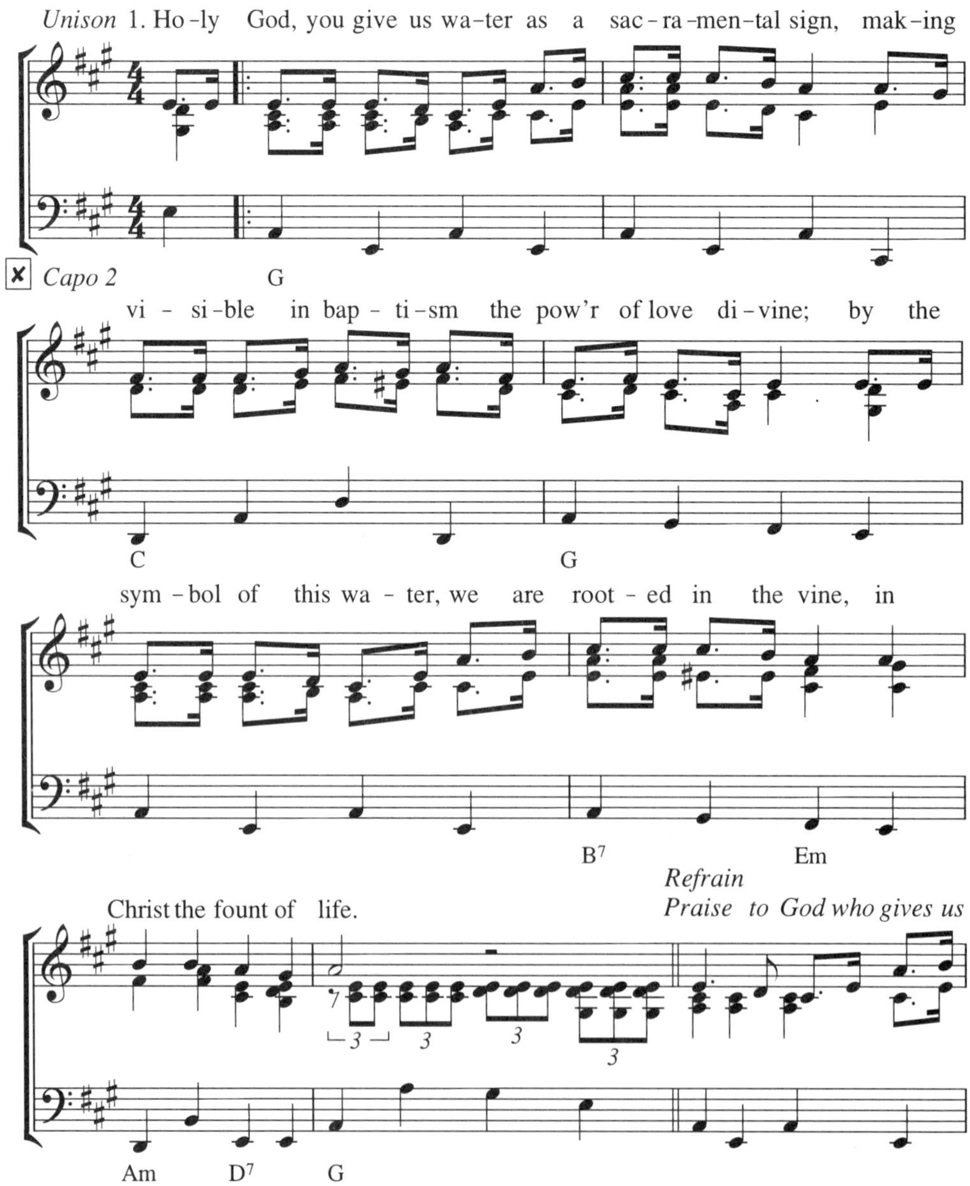

2 At the dawning of creation,
as you breathed the living word,
by the movement of your spirit
were the primal waters stirred,
and gave birth to new creation
when your call to life was heard,
let life begin anew.

3 Through the waters of the flood,
and by the parting of the sea,
you have cleansed us and renewed us,
called us out and set us free,
as in baptism the slaves of sin
receive their liberty;
let us now journey on.

4 In the waters of the Jordan
Christ was glad to be baptised,
and anointed with the Spirit's
pow'r before the people's eyes,
so from overwhelming waters,
still, he bids our spirits rise,
may we be blessed in Christ.

5 Jesus thirsted after righteousness
and justice as he died,
and he poured out blood and water
from the spear wound in his side,
so in baptism the church of Christ
is born and unified,
may Christ's death give us life.

6 Both in sacrament and word
has Christ commissioned us anew
to make known his living presence
by the things we say and do,
to go out to every nation
and bear witness to his truth,
may all be one in Christ.

The priest says the prayer of blessing, and the congregation respond with the final verse:

7 Though the floods of death engulfed him
in despondency and gloom,
Though his body was confined
within the darkness of the tomb,
yet the freedom of Christ's Spirit
turned the grave into a womb!
We rise from death to life!

Text: Michael Forster (b. 1946)
Music: traditional American arr. Christopher Tambling

Renewal of Baptismal Vows and Sprinkling with Baptismal Water

After the candidates (if there are any) have been initiated, everyone in the congregation is invited to renew their baptismal commitment. This could be complemented by their being sprinkled with baptismal water.

However, their verbal assertion of reaffirmation could be more powerfully expressed, not by the *passive* gesture of being sprinkled, but by the *active* gesture of coming forward in procession, to plunge their hand in the font and make the sign of the cross on their forehead. Such a positive gesture is surely more symbolic of the personal commitment to renewal.

If the proclamation of the scriptural texts and psalms has been effective, the people will have their heads full of images of saving water. The complementary physical contact with water helps to underline the reality of the saving mystery into which they have been plunged by their baptism.

Whether the assembly is invited to come forward, or whether the people remain in their pews to be sprinkled, this contact with water should be accompanied by a song which is baptismal in character. If 'Holy God, you give us water' (page 88) was not used for the prayer of blessing, it could be used now.

Alternatively, here is a metrical paraphrase of Ephesians 1, which is a song of thanksgiving to God for having adopted us as his children and heirs in Christ through baptism. Notice how fully it expresses the mystery of baptism: not just being made children of God, but the forgiveness of sins, incorporation into Christ, and the seal of the Spirit. The use of the majestic tune *Old Hundredth* should help underline the notion of the royal priesthood in which we share through baptism (see 1 Peter 2:9).

OLD HUNDREDTH LM (All people that on earth do dwell)

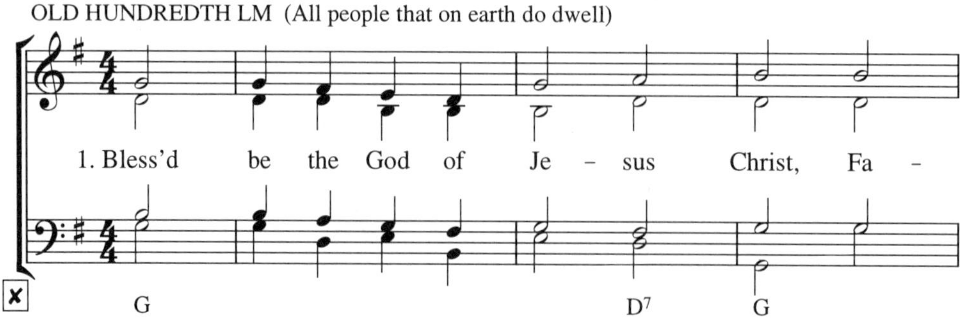

2
Chosen in Christ, by God's good will,
before the earth was set in place,
called to be children of his love,
and holy stand before his face:

3
We have redemption through his blood,
pardon by his abundant grace,
blessings eternal from above,
made known by Christ in time and
space.

4
Wisdom and insight of our God
make known the myst'ry of his ways;
to him all things of heav'n and earth
shall gather on the final day.

5
In him the gospel truth is known,
his word of wholeness is revealed.
All who believe and trust in him
are with the Holy Spirit sealed.

6
This is the pledge that we receive,
sign of redemption as his own;
then shall the heav'ns and earth unite
to make his praise and glory known.

Text: Michael Forster (b. 1946)
Music: from the *Genevan Psalter* (1551)

LITURGY OF THE EUCHARIST

Song during the Preparation of the Gifts and the Altar

We prepare the altar and we present our gifts. We do so because we are baptised: because we constitute a priestly people, we are now able to stand round the altar, and celebrate the sacrament of the eucharist. We dare to do so only because we are the people of God, won by Christ with his blood, called together by the Lord. The song sung during this preparation could reflect on this: if 'Bless'd be the God of Jesus Christ' was not used for the sprinkling song (see page 90) it would be appropriate now.

At the Breaking of the Bread (Agnus Dei)

Here again is the *Agnus Dei* that has been with us throughout Holy Week. Tonight's central verse goes beyond the image of Christ as Paschal Lamb, the first to die and rise, to celebrate him as Shepherd for his people, leading us through the same Paschal Mystery. So, as we proclaimed when marking the candle, Christ is our beginning and our end.

REPTON 86 88 6 (Dear Lord and Father of mankind)

2
O Lamb of God, as Shepherd, tend
the souls of us who stray.
Our true beginning and our end,
the myst'ry none can comprehend,
O hear us when we pray,
O hear us when we pray.

3
O Lamb of God, our lives restore,
our guilty souls release.
Into our lives your Spirit pour,
and let us live for evermore
in perfect heav'nly peace,
in perfect heav'nly peace.

Text: Michael Forster (b. 1946)
Music: Hubert Parry (1848-1918)

SEE OVERLEAF FOR EASY
COPYRIGHT CLEARANCE

Please photocopy this page

KEVIN MAYHEW EASY COPYRIGHT CLEARANCE

All the hymns in this book are copyright and must not be reproduced in any way without the proper permission.

Kevin Mayhew Ltd is a member of the Christian Copyright Licensing scheme, and the words of these hymns may be reproduced by those churches possessing a Church Copyright Licence. Please make sure that you enter the titles on your annual returns. Further information may be obtained from Christian Copyright Licensing Ltd, 26 Gildredge Avenue, Eastbourne, East Sussex BN21 4SA. Alternatively, a one-year licence to reproduce some or all of these hymns for non-commercial use may be obtained from the Kevin Mayhew Copyright Department by sending a copy of this page together with your payment.

Name of Church ______________________________

Contact Name ______________________________

Address ______________________________

____

Postcode ______________________________

Telephone Number ______________________________

Fax Number ______________________________

The hymn(s) you intend to copy: Page(s) ______________________________

Fees for one-year licence

£4.70 per hymn. This fee is valid until 31 December 1997. After that date please contact the Copyright Department for information.

Fee due: ________ hymn(s) at £4.70 each Total ______________________________

Please enclose payment by cheque or fill in the details of your Visa / Mastercard number below.

Expiry date until end ________________

Signed ______________________________

To be completed by Kevin Mayhew Ltd

Payment of £ ________ received. Thank you.

Permission is granted subject to the following further conditions:

1. that the author is acknowledged on every copy.
2. that the following copyright line is included on every copy:

   Copyright Kevin Mayhew Ltd. Reproduced by permission
   from *This is the Feast.*
   Licence Number ______________________________

This Licence expires on: ______________________________

Signed for Kevin Mayhew Ltd ______________________________

Copyright Department, Kevin Mayhew Ltd, Rattlesden, Bury St Edmunds, Suffolk IP30 0SZ
Telephone number: UK 01449 737978 International +44 1449 737978
Fax number: UK 01449 737834 International +44 1449 737834